Ricochet

Also by Carl Vigeland

Great Good Fortune: How Harvard Makes It Money
In Concert: Onstage and Offstage with the Boston Symphony Orchestra
Stalking the Shark: Pressure and Passion on the Pro Golf Tour
Jazz in the Bittersweet Blues of Life (with Wynton Marsalis)
Letters to a Young Golfer (with Bob Duval)
The Mostly Mozart Guide to Mozart
The Breathless Present: A Memoir in Four Movements
Jonathan Sternberg
The Great Romance: The Sun Returns, Time Never
A Symphony for Shelbie
Dear President Trump: An Open Letter on Greatness
French Lessons (with Joseph C. French Jr.)
October Calf (with Archibald MacLeish)
Walking Trane

Carl Vigeland

RICOCHET

Combray House

Copyright © 2021 Carl Vigeland

All right reserved. No part of this publication may be reproduced, stored in a retrieval system, or transmitted, in any form or by any means, electronic, mechanical, photocopying, recording, or otherwise, without the prior written permission of the publisher at www.combrayhousebooks.com. A shorter version of *Ricochet* was published previously as part of a different book by Levellers Press; an excerpt was published in *Massachusetts Review*.

Cover by Jim Madden/Asterisk Design; center cover photograph by Frank Stewart; right cover photo by Christian Vigeland; back cover photo by Anna Vigeland; photo on dedication page by the author.

ISBN 978-1-7362292-0-0

for Maren

Contents

Prologue	11
I Chord Changes	13
II Home and Away	50
III Blues for My Father	109
IV Blowing Beauty	167
V Ricochet	257
Epilogue	268
Acknowledgments	273

Prologue

"Life is long," Wynton Marsalis said to me in 1991, after I had flown to New Orleans to join his septet for a short tour, which I expected would form the setting and provide much of the subject matter for a book we had agreed to do. Ten years passed before that book was finally published, by which time I had visited almost every state and twice been overseas with an artist whose career has no parallel in the history of music.

I first met Wynton in 1989, not far from my home in western Massachusetts. My father, also a musician, had died a few years earlier; my third child, a daughter named Maren, had just been born. Our lives move through a complex of criss-crossing arcs, and so it was that I found myself on a late November day in 2003 in a hall where my father had once played the organ, the interweaving themes and harmonies of the music inspiring within me a counterpoint of loss and longing.

"Emotions are a constant integration and improvisation of what one is feeling, not just one or two emotions," a close friend of Wynton's once wrote me. "*I love or not love,*" *goes pop music;* "*I move or not move; I fly or not fly; the moon is yellow or bright and the garden is lovely tonight,*" *she said. Ask anyone, do they just want to make love or would they like to have technique and lots of emotions? When you are baptized, you don't think, "Am I going to drown or not drown?" You are just filled with joy.*

I
Chord Changes

"If I were going to read a story," Maren said as we walked Jack on a cold, gray November afternoon, "I wouldn't want to read it if you could explain the story in a couple of sentences. I would only want to read a story if you had to read all of it to understand it." Maren had been sick much of the fall, with mono her doctor thought, but the test results kept coming back negative. She'd missed a lot of school. We had just been to her school to get work she was supposed to make up. Now we were walking Jack in the gathering dusk, with a brisk wind whipping the chilly air against our faces. The soccer field next to the football stadium was littered with cups and food wrappings from a football function the previous weekend. Jack sniffed at the stuff as he looked for a place to pee.

What would I need to say if I were going to write the story my daughter described, a story you could read late at night in a quiet corner of the city somewhere? What words would find the feeling of that summer day when I took off—went on the road—certain this was something I had to do as I kissed my children goodbye, Maren the youngest still sleeping with the calendar I'd bought her on the wall by her bed, each trip the days I would be gone marked off so she could see? Little did I imagine then how many more days, weeks, months...years until the Boston performances in Symphony Hall of a piece called *All Rise*: the accelerating energy of those men and women as they came on stage for the final rehearsal, their different lives, where they might have been the night before and with whom they had made love. And then, slowly making his way across the stage, the architect of that day's musical activity, Wynton Marsalis, whom I first met more than a decade earlier, the year Maren was born, and who repeatedly said his ambition was "to be part of something great," by which he meant jazz, Wynton who once told me that if he had to he could live happily in his old Louisiana neighborhood, passing the time on the stoop of his house, listening to the music of his neighbors' voices while watching the passage of an old couple and a pretty girl down a dusty, unpaved street.

Relaxed, deliberate in his manner, Wynton shook hands that December morning with a few of the musicians whom he passed, stopping to talk familiarly with one of the Boston orchestra's trumpet players, a proud, tenacious, silver-haired man who nearly lost his job 20 years ago after a prolonged fight with his music director, before finally taking a seat with his big band, which was surrounded by all the other instrumental musicians and a chorus behind them on a giant stage in an historic hall that I first visited with my father half a century ago. I was four or five years old then and my father—"a keyboard musician, just like my Daddy," Wynton would sometimes say by way of explaining to others one of the things he said we had in common—long tormented by competing forces of guilt and pleasure and dead now more than 20 years, played Symphony Hall's new pipe organ on a sunlit day I would remember more for the ride we took later on one of Boston's famous swan boats and the smile I can still sense on my father's deeply expressive face because his family was young, his career ascendant.

What would Maren make of my memory of a man who died seven years before her birth, the grandfather she never knew?

And what would she think about the old lady from the audience in Lincoln, Nebraska who accepted Wynton's invitation there to sit on stage with the band and when Wynton named the musicians at the end of the gig introduced her as well and she proudly stood and accepting the applause took a bow. Or Harold Russell in his tee shirt with the Marlboros in a tucked sleeve and Darleen sitting in the seat behind the driver's, behind Harold, when she came out one week—we were in Colorado and Wyoming that week—it was her vacation, and also her birthday, and one quiet morning in Laramie, the air still as an arrow ready to be pulled, we walked the town, along Main Street over to the deserted old train station, Darleen and Harold holding hands and talking animatedly, "Look at that, Harold, that store selling cowboy hats. Wouldn't you look handsome in one."

Wyoming was vast and made me feel small, fearful that I might never understand the complex of relationships that bound me by then to a trumpet player from New Orleans and a chain-smoking pit bull—Wynton's words—from Tennessee who used to drive for Guns 'N Roses and wore a John Mellencamp leather jacket that girls, he said, had propositioned him for, Harold who spoke to me with tears in his eyes after the road life caught up to him, a doctor told him he had to quit driving, and I asked Harold following lunch in a barbecue place as we talked in his rented retirement condo—he and Darleen had moved to Colorado Springs—what was it about music that mattered?

"The people," he said, and Darleen, looking up from the coffee she was making us, shook her head and softly said, "Harold." He called her his treasure, with the cute smile and the Harlequin romance in her lap when she used to come out on the road and in her eyes a deep longing that Harold returned after parking the bus and locking it for the night and started talking about the petite woman who worked in Tennessee back when Harold was on the road, so that they often went weeks without seeing one another. How did Harold sleep I sometimes wondered, alone, with his cigarette cough and the hours on the road, often driving all night and then through much of the next day, crisscrossing America so many times he knew the whole country like a map..."After three million miles," he wrote me, "I was the best damn driver I have ever met! During that three million I kept looking for him. I was it all along!"—knew every shortcut around every downtown and where the cops were waiting to ticket and how the weather changed in the mountains, knew the way from Laramie to Cheyenne, which is where we were headed that time on Darleen's birthday, buffalo grazing in a pasture and the sky low over the hills with clouds and an ominous sense of enclosure, like a curtain coming down, that whole vast place a stage.

And there's Wess Anderson in the bus putting on some music, getting his horn out too, Wess with the sweet voice and the sweeter sound, and in those days still the cigarettes, so he always sat in the front of the bus as if that made a difference with his smoking, Wess with the very dark oval face with its soft features and the way his eyebrows furrowed as he listened and you felt underneath the cheerfulness the hollow hurt of his sister's death, he was in a nightclub playing when his wife Desi came in to tell him she had been shot, and also the little catch in his voice when he was maybe sitting at a bar, laughing, listening to you, how he always asked me by name how each person in my family was and when I said the same to him he always said *Des is fine, Quad is fine,* but as we locked one another in our eyes I sometimes wondered, "Should you really me trust me, do I deserve your affection?" And how might I answer my own question, by what right could I answer, *the noble Norseman*, Wynton jokingly referred to me once from the stage at a club in Monterrey, California, *Mass*, as in *Massa*, he often called me when he had his plantation vibe going in the bus or on the ride from hotel to venue, and afterwards I might think, as I stood off to the side in the dressing room: *the token cracker*.

    In this story I would put how the April air smells on the Dakota plains, how I once walked down a dirt road to the edge of a huge manmade reservoir there on the Missouri River and placed my hand in the water which was cold because winter lasts so long on the prairie, the ground was still frozen in places, the grass sere, and in my head I heard a Wyntonian tune, *Superb Starling*, which I felt certain could be played at either a wedding or a funeral, same song, because it was both happy and sad, not just one emotion but many, integrated in their improvisation. How I loved the prairie grass in summer, with the music a kind of backdrop, or maybe literally a soundtrack, just as it was in Boston for that November *All Rise*.

Over Thanksgiving, we had just visited with my mother, sick since summer with one ailment leading to another, now bedridden in a Bronxville, New York hospital. Would I put that in my story, too? In her hospital room she and I had watched part of *American Beauty* on DVD and I'd given her some jazz I knew she probably would not listen to ("Why can't he just stick with the melody?" she would ask when I played her one of Wynton's many versions of his favorite song, Gershwin's *Embraceable You*). She was frail but alert. As I left her in the hospital the day after Thanksgiving, the late afternoon light already disappearing into dusk, I had bumped into her doctor, a woman not much younger than my mother. Reviewing my mother's charts in the hallway near my mother's room, she had removed her glasses before speaking to me in a highly inflected English with the trace of an Austrian or German accent, shaking her head as if to emphasize the element of mystery in any prognosis, and then without any prompting on my part had said, looking directly into my eyes, "You have to seize life."

Walking outside then in the chilly, leaf-scented November air, I had looked for the cafe we'd all been to on an earlier visit, when my mom had still been able to walk. Couldn't find it so I'd continued past the stucco train station and down a block where the lights were on in the marquee of the old movie theater near Bronxville's Starbucks.

The traffic that had made it difficult to park in Bronxville before visiting my mother had subsided, but the sidewalk by Starbucks was still bustling. An old man walking his poodle reminded me of Jack; it was just a week since Maren and I had stopped with Jack that afternoon at the football field and talked about books while he peed. Maren had asked on this visit to go into the city to see Wynton but had happily settled for an afternoon of food shopping in the Bronx's little Italy with my brother, who knew many of the shopkeepers, greeting them by name as he bought bread at a bakery that sold only bread and ravioli at a pasta shop that had been run by the same family since the 1930s and carried only the ravioli it made in the back room.

Not knowing if I would find my mother alive the next morning, I had looked for her room's window in the hospital as I walked from Starbucks to my car. Breathing quietly, she had been asleep already when I kissed her forehead and departed. I pictured that breathing as I stared momentarily at her window, a sense of the space she still occupied on the earth, everywhere people breathing, all the while the earth spinning, and then I left.

Gazing out at the post-Thanksgiving, early winter light in Boston as I waited after an *All Rise* rehearsal for the van that would take us back to the hotel, I remembered that it was almost the exact time of year that Wynton had invited me more than a decade ago to come to Boston with him and his septet after I'd heard them play a second time at the Iron Horse Café in Northampton, Massachusetts.

"Ride with us on our bus," Wynton had suggested then, during a post-gig, midnight game of basketball, outdoors, in a parking lot located between his Northampton motel and the interstate. It was less an invitation than a command.

"Thanks," I had replied, feigning a relaxed tone. "I have family stuff in the morning," I continued. "I'll drive."

The next afternoon, a few minutes after I

arrived in Boston, we had gone to a sound check at Berklee College of Music, my first ride in a limousine, and on the way back we were accompanied by Matt Dillon—"Monyure," a bastardized form of Monsieur, he was called within the band—a short, wiry-haired, sharp-tongued energetic man, a New Orleans childhood friend of Wynton's who was Wynton's road manager at that time. This was before he became a Baskin and Robbins ice cream impresario at the airport in his hometown, while living alone across the Mississippi Rivers in Algiers (where Buddy Bolden a century ago was reputed to blow his horn so loud you could hear it on Canal Street), in a small, trim house filled with memorabilia from his road days—days when he thought the touring life would always continue, the nice hotels and good crowds, adoring fans, meals like the one in Monterrey at a Mexican restaurant where they opened early for the band and prepared a few special dishes...days like that in Boston when in the limo Matt had told jokes and reminisced rhapsodically with Wynton about the beauty and sexual attraction of different New Orleans women.

Back at the hotel then, Wynton felt the top of his head, looked in a mirror, and announced that he needed a haircut. So I had accompanied him and a large white guy from Buffalo named Wes, one 's,' who was hanging with the band that tour, gone along with them to a barbershop a few blocks from the hotel in what was still a mostly Black neighborhood in Boston's South End.

On a table at the barbershop was a copy of a recent *Time* Magazine with Wynton on the cover. Though I would learn he shunned such terms as creations of "the media," Wynton was then at a kind of crossroads in his young career, something the *Time* article worked around. Already at the age of 29 world famous, the recipient of numerous awards including eight Grammys, he had only just a few years earlier gone through a personal and musical crisis when his brother Branford left his band. Just a year apart at birth, they had grown up together, and played music together at home with their father Ellis, a pianist, at the school, the New Orleans Center for the Creative Arts, that Ellis had helped found, and in the funk band, the Creators, they formed as teenagers. Branford's defection had been a rebuke, made worse in Wynton's eyes because his older brother had departed to play with a British pop star, Sting. It was something Wynton rarely discussed; we would have only one extended conversation about it, in Shreveport, Louisiana, the first fall after I began touring with him, when the initial hurt seemed to be softening into the realization that perhaps the brothers were better off playing on their own. Emerging from the loss, which also included that of two other players in his old quintet, Wynton had gradually formed a new band which, with the addition of trombonist Wycliffe Gordon, had in 1989 become a septet. This was the group which I would hear that same year when I first encountered Wynton and his music in person in Northampton's Iron Horse Café, and it was the septet that had just appeared again a year later at the Iron Horse.

The barber in Boston fussed over Wynton, and didn't want to take any money, but Wynton insisted on paying. Then he reached into his pocket and discovered he had only a few singles on him. He almost never carried more in those days, money being something he did not think about in the sense of what a gallon of milk or loaf of bread cost.

"Hey, bruh, can you take care of my man here," he must have said to Wes, though I didn't hear.

Returning from his haircut to his hotel suite, which overlooked the Boston Common, Wynton talked on the phone with his two young sons , Wynton Jr. and Simeon, who were with their mother, Candace Stanley, in New York. Wynton lived there, too, with them still, in a lower Manhattan brownstone, during the rare weeks when he wasn't traveling.

I had taken a seat at a baby grand piano that had been placed in a corner of the suite's living room; there was usually a piano wherever Wynton stayed, even if the band were in a hotel that had to arrange a rental. Waiting for Wynton, I watched the holiday lights on the Common and studied the neatly penciled manuscript for the beginning of what I was later certain was his Pulitzer Prize-winning slavery oratorio *Blood on the Fields,* though he would always insist otherwise. The music looked at once familiar and foreign to me, just as hearing the band the night before had seemed on the one hand the kind of musical event I had experienced countless times and on the other hand something very different, even exotic.

Somewhat self-consciously, I studied the manuscript, but it felt comfortable to be sitting there at the piano. My own piano studies had started when I was five, and I added the trumpet at the age of nine. Growing up in Buffalo, New York, where for several years my father managed the orchestra, I had always been surrounded by music and musicians. The eccentric pianist Glenn Gould came to a reception in his honor at our home, standing on a heating grate in our living room, where for a time there were two concert grand pianos, and wearing gloves, refused to shake anyone's hand lest he pick up germs. A few blocks from our house was a club called the Royal Arms, where I once listened to pianist Ramsey Lewis while I stood outside, peering through the window, since I wasn't old enough to enter the club legally. I heard Louis Armstrong play in person shortly before he died, at an outdoor theater under a tent on a gig that ended with numerous encores. I did not understand who Armstrong was, and there were many jazz musicians whose music I did not know, but I never forgot that night, how at the age of 70, "Pops" came out again and again for encores.

Long before it became fashionable in conservatories and music festivals to acknowledge this, my father—the son of Norwegian immigrants, raised in a strict, socially closed, fundamentalist environment by parents who called the Negroes living in Harlem *the chocolata*—taught me by example that Duke Ellington was an important musical figure. My dad, who studied at Juilliard when he was in high school and was only 17 or 18 when he left home for the Berkshires, had a stained glass window of Duke put in at the church where he was organist. I can still remember the excitement in my father's voice when, on a visit to me in college, he said while we were having breakfast in the dining room at his hotel, "Look behind you!

That's Duke Ellington at the table in the alcove."

Except for rock and roll and most atonal and serial compositions, even music my father didn't particularly like still merited a certain respect. And music he loved—all of Bach, most of Mozart, Debussy, Vaughn Williams (whose *Fantasy on a Theme of Thomas Tallis*, we were told, he wanted to be played at his funeral), and Mahler—aroused in him a kind of passionate fervor bordering on religious. How often had I come home late at night when I was still in high school to find my father in a trance listening to Mahler's *Ruckert Lieder* or one of his favorite Bach chorales. It was only in such music that my father seemed able, albeit temporarily, to abate or assuage the angers and griefs of a life that included not only the early death of his brother but constant worries about money, as if the music's struggles mirrored his own, his very salvation dependent on its triumph, however seemingly tenuous at times, over his terrors. Music for my father at those moments when he was truly hearing it *was* life—just as I imagined it was for my new friend from New Orleans, except in his case the words seemed reversible, or interchangeable. His life, this amazing combination of constant travel and performance, the rhythm of its movement and the counterpoint of its interactions with others, was a kind of music.

After Wynton had said goodnight to his sons on the phone at the Park Plaza he came over to the piano bench and played the music I had been staring at, just the first few chords, lush, taut, evocative. Years afterwards, when I told someone this story in Wynton's presence, he was annoyed that I repeated a misidentification of the music he played then, the way he once told me his mother would sometimes ask him a question he'd already answered or tell him something he already knew or she'd already said. Where were we during that conversation? West Virginia? Texas?

"I explained to you it was something else," I can hear him saying impatiently.

It was a long time before I learned to let these complaints go. They invariably meant nothing, or were said only to provoke for the fun of the provocation. Once he told me a woman he knew I thought was cute, who was also my friend, had come to see him one night in New York and...he looked at me with a wild grin, his eyes brightening, before breaking into laughter, no longer able to maintain the pose. Months later when I quizzed him he insisted they had never even kissed.

So, Skain, what are you really trying to tell me? It was a question that, after years of traveling with his bands, I would ask myself often. Reading a mood, Wynton anticipated how someone else might react to what he said. In a debate (and what conversation with Wynton was not a debate?), he was artful at keeping an opponent off balance, just like a good athlete in his favorite sport, boxing. He knew how to needle. But he also understood the power of a seemingly offhand remark. One time—this was in New York—we were walking to a Lincoln Center gig and I told him I had been listening to the outtakes from his *In This House, On This Morning*, one of the first extended pieces he had written, and of all his compositions the one I still love the best.

"The second half, right from the moment Veal starts to sing, is so beautiful," I said. "The whole thing, right to the end."

"You didn't like the first half?" Wynton responded.

His apparent refusal to accept my compliment threw me off balance, and I was left to backtrack, which made me sound foolish. But I was also struck by the transparency of his remark. Was this man who came across as so sure of everything he felt exposing a momentary uncertainty? Or was he just playing with me again?

"Yeah, Squazene, that first half was truly sad. When are you going to write some music that has some real feeling to it?"

*

Boston these many years afterwards was cold outside and crowded with shoppers. Returning to the hotel following the rehearsal, the van stopped to let off baritone saxophonist Joe Temperley at a restaurant, Legal Seafood. Glancing out the window at people with their coat collars turned up, I laughed quietly at a joke someone made about the name of the restaurant. You never laughed—or cried, or for that matter spoke—loudly in the company of the band, a lesson I'd learned from another of my road tutors, soundman David Robinson, who used to mock my high-pitched laugh and who, like Monyure Dillon (or erstwhile road managers Brother Elie and Billy Banks, or their present successor Boss Murphy), did not actually play an instrument in any of Wynton's bands but was still accorded full status as a member of whichever of his groups Wynton was touring with: the septet that had formed after the departure of Branford; Wynton's big band, officially the Lincoln Center Jazz Orchestra, which was started in the early 1990s and included many of the septet's musicians; or a third group, a quartet comprised of Wynton and three much younger players which appeared later, following the diminution of a reconstituted septet. Even people who had no formal association with Wynton were made to feel part of the ensemble while they were on the road; there were no outsiders in this world. I had certainly come to know that.

As we left Joe off, the darkening day mirrored my mood, melancholy over the cessation of the music and always vaguely uneasy over the prospect of something happening in my absence at home, and I strained to hear in my memory snippets of the chorus at the rehearsal singing in great intervals, and then a place in the music that dissolved with the wail of the saxophone, except I wasn't thinking in sections, it was as if I were listening to the entire 100-minute piece at once. I imagined a movie and it would be the piece as written but performed both on stage and where the music had taken me. It would be a kind of music video, but large scale, with lots of people in it, including the performers, and also all sorts of people on the road, the people you meet on the road through music.

The beginning was in the mountains somewhere, and then that first part continued in some cities; the section for strings in the west, or Appalachia; the moment I was listening to played against the Golden Gate at dawn, the sunlit morning several years ago when Wynton and photographer Frank Stewart and I crossed it on our way from Santa Rosa to the airport, the night after Frank and I drank cognac we found in a little store in the strip mall by our motel, while Wynton in the next room dealt with the heartbreak of a pianist he was sending home, and that morning we were flying to New Mexico, where after performing and being honored at a native American Gathering of Nations Wynton would finish writing the recessional of *In This House, On This Morning* in the shadow of the mountains that guarded Albuquerque. I remembered his playing on a miniature piano in his hotel room a refrain in the unusual, technically difficult rhythm of 7/4 (seven beats to a measure, a quarter note gets a beat), so when I left for home the next morning the refrain was still in my head as I looked out at the same mountains, their tops covered in clouds, and ever after when I have heard the harmonics of that figure over that mesmerizing rhythm I have seen that vista, felt the clear desert air as if it were soothing my life.

Like chord changes in the music, one memory now triggered another as we waited in Boston for a traffic light to turn: little more than a year before, on a cool, cloudy early autumn day in nearby New Hampshire, Wynton announced matter-of-factly during a pre-concert dinner that his grandmother had just died. We were eating in a pine-paneled basement room of the Hanover Inn, a room with a WASPy vibe reminiscent of other Dartmouth places in the old black and white movie, *Winter Carnival*. At the gig that night, the hall packed with elderly blue hairs, many of the men wearing jackets and ties and most of the women in dresses, Wynton was unusually reserved backstage during intermission, but then played a highly charged duet, a spontaneous performance of *St. James Infirmary* with Wess Anderson on the piano, the instrument Wess had learned from his father before Wess became a saxophonist. Though Wynton said nothing about his grandmother from the stage, and would have denied any connection—"I play the same," he always said—it was difficult not to hear the duet as a tribute to her.

I'd driven to that gig at the last minute, meeting the band at the Hanover Inn just as everyone was walking next door to the venue for a sound check followed by supper, the kind of serendipitous timing that tended to occur frequently in my road life, and not until we returned to the hotel did I notice I had come all this way wearing my bedroom slippers. Without comment or question, but shaking his head as if to chastise a child, Wynton loaned me a pair of perfectly polished shoes. When I returned them after the gig I mentioned my response to the duet with Wess. At first Wynton feigned the kind of ignorance of a performance's impact that he often assumed.

"Did we sound like shit?" he asked.

"Yeah, right," I said, though I rarely knew what to reply in such instances, since criticism for its own sake was gratuitous and the truth often came across as cheesy. What you "thought" about a particular piece seemed far less important than understanding why what you heard made you feel. It was the same being on the road, except there the initial question turned on experience, what actually happened in a particular instance, and then once again what was the relationship to how you felt?

At Dartmouth that night, I changed the subject to a student named Kabir Sehgal who earlier had presented to Wynton medals for him and the rest of the band that a group Kabir was a part of designed to commemorate this concert. Wynton publicly acknowledged Kabir, who was also a bass player, by inviting him to join the septet on the last tune. The house had emptied quickly afterwards, finally leaving only a family that had driven two hours from northern New Hampshire so their very young son, a trumpeter himself, could meet Wynton. Though it was getting late, for half an hour Wynton had played some blues on the piano while encouraging the boy, who was quite talented, to solo on the horn he had brought along with him. In more than one similar exchange that I had witnessed over the years the upshot was a call from whomever Wynton had just helped to Wynton's longtime manager, Ed Arrendell, whom Wynton would have told a student or student's parents to contact because a boy or girl could not afford music lessons, or in at least one especially notable instance because financial aid at a particular music camp was unavailable. Wynton, who had grown up in an economically struggling Black family in the South and whose only real indulgence were his musicians (much of what he made he spent on his band) and his elegant clothes, would pay.

Money was only a means to an end for Wynton. In his apartment there were relatively few possessions: some paintings, a stereo one of his brothers gave him, his piano. Music. Books. Children's toys, when his sons were little. He didn't have many trumpets either, just the one he was currently playing, a decorated horn, a piccolo trumpet for baroque music, and a cornet. He gave his old trumpets away, to students and friends. Nicholas Payton from New Orleans had one, the same Nicholas for whose high school graduation Wynton flew all the way from New York to attend, the kind of gesture he made for his sons whenever it was even remotely possible, such as the time after a gig in Cleveland when he drove all night to be in New York for an event at his son Simeon's junior high.

More chord changes: I had been rereading Ralph Ellison, and as I listened to the boy in New Hampshire play his blues I remembered the place, central Florida, when Wynton introduced me to Ellison's *Little Man at Chehaw Station*. We were on the bus, Wynton, I, and Matt Dillon's replacement Lolis Elie, another New Orleans childhood friend of Wynton's, a writer between gigs, variously called Brother Elie or, by me, Reverend—because he had preached a mock sermon, which concluded with a baptismal invocation for my unlikely deliverance on Judgment Day, at a dinner party in North Carolina. On the bus in Florida as we came into Orlando, Wynton had read aloud some of the Ellison essay, which expounded on the proposition that you never knew who might be listening (or watching, or wondering).

Before the New Hampshire gig I had gone back to the Ellison because I had just seen the Little Man, except that he was a she: a young woman I knew through her father, a college classmate of mine, who had been living abroad since her own graduation from college a few years ago. Early that past summer she was badly hurt after a fire triggered an explosion in the house where she was sleeping and she was unable to escape immediately. She almost died then, and later she almost died a second time, of an embolism, in an airplane en route to a hospital in Boston. Now she was continuing her treatment but she had her life back, and despite the scars a radiance that was breathtaking. While she was still in the hospital I learned from her father that she had discovered jazz, and when she came home finally I gave her a few of Wynton's CDs, *Majesty of the Blues* and a couple of others. Some time passed, and then one day I received a note from her, illustrated by a drawing of Wynton she had done based on the photo in the *Majesty* liner notes.

"Throughout my recovery I have found music and art to be an incredibly powerful form of therapeutic healing," she wrote in a hand so striking it resembled calligraphy, "a creative expression which (as Marsalis notes) is a testament to the strength of the human spirit." Soon afterwards I saw her by chance in town, and then again a few days later at the local HMO, and all she could talk about was music. I arranged to get tickets for her to attend a gig Wynton was giving the following spring.

She came backstage to meet Wynton then but had to leave almost immediately because her parents were waiting to give her a ride. Though he had earlier listened to my reading of her heartfelt note without external reaction, Wynton asked me afterwards in the hotel where she was. The room smelled of cleaning spray, and a fan made a loud whirring noise, but Wynton seemed not to notice. Tired, he was already lying in his bed, almost nodding off.

"She had to go," I replied. "She gets tired. She's still recovering."

"She was sweet," Wynton said. "I think she wanted to stay," he continued.

Because I had known this young woman since she was a girl, I felt protective about her, and Wynton's remark struck me as self-centered. And yet, as I imagined the moment after the explosion when the woman was trapped in the burning building and the pain of that seared flesh, the agony of her long recovery and the gradual realization of what she had lost, I was less certain. Perhaps her beauty had inspired him to speak a truth my reticence had kept me from admitting.

Though it was rare that Wynton ever truly forget something, especially a name (especially the name of a beautiful woman), he pleaded ignorance about what he'd said that night when I mentioned it to him a few months later. He was appearing in the same Northampton club where I had first met him, this time with a small group of much younger musicians who were to form his new quartet. On the first date of a double engagement an especially youthful-looking musician had shown up between sets with a piccolo trumpet to play the Second Brandenburg Concerto of Bach. After Wynton with a kind voice bluntly asked this earnest student if he knew the meaning of the word nuance, Wynton wiped off the piccolo trumpet's mouthpiece to clean it a little and then, adjusting his embouchure, launched into the Bach right there, an impromptu, hair-raising performance of a piece that had helped propel him years ago to prominence but that he no longer played in public.

On the second night of the same gig, again between sets, a petite young woman named Sally appeared to sing. Sally had driven two hours to the club, having apparently called ahead to say she was coming. I didn't know where they had met, and Wynton certainly didn't say. He rarely provided such information spontaneously, and never when asked. Sally was studying voice and she'd prepared *Autumn Leaves* for Wynton, which for some reason she sang in French. She had a sweet if tentative voice; she was clearly nervous.

"Sing some blues," Wynton requested.

Taken aback, Sally tried to recall a song that would satisfy Wynton's request. There was an awkward silence that Wynton broke with his tenor, no words, just the mimicked sounds of a bass fiddle being plucked. He was showing Sally what he meant, singing in the form of a blues. Relieved, she got the idea and began when he paused. Her singing was somewhat self-conscious but she kept the form. Pianist Eric Lewis, who had been listening to this unofficial audition from a corner of the room, now came over and, standing, facing Sally, with his own voice picked up the bass part from Wynton, who then grabbed his trumpet and provided an accompaniment. The singing and playing continued like this uninterrupted for a full 15 or 20 minutes, until someone stuck his head in the door and said, "House is ready." Wynton smiled at Sally, took her hand, said with a pronounced pause between each word, "Practice…the…blues," and walked upstairs to play his second set.

It was raining hard by the time he left the club two hours later. The hotel was only a couple of blocks away, but Boss Murphy had brought the tour bus around, so we wouldn't get wet. At the hotel I walked Wynton to his room, where we talked for a little while — he asked about my kids, particularly Maren, whom he had known since she was an infant. Then there was a knock on the door and in came Sally. She was carrying a small bag.

I got up, but Wynton said, "Don't leave, Swig. It's not what you think." Sally had told him she was driving home in the rain, Wynton declared, and he had invited her to sleep here, in his room, and leave in the morning when the driving would be safer. He wouldn't even be there by then; the tour bus was going at four.

While Sally disappeared into the bathroom, I stayed a few more minutes, and then, having changed into some tights and a top, she reappeared, smiled, said something about the gig and the rain and, hearing part of our conversation, picked up on my daughter's name, and quickly climbed onto the double bed. She got under the covers, thanked Wynton for his hospitality, and was soon apparently fast asleep.

While an air of heightened expectation almost always animated a scene in which Wynton encountered a woman, what struck me most was the ease with which he moved in and out of most relationships, whether brief encounters such as this one with Sally or long-lasting ones. Just about a year before, Wynton's first New Orleans girlfriend, Melanie Marchand, had celebrated her 40th birthday with him at a hotel bar in Harrisburg, Pennsylvania, where Wynton jokingly shared memories of their meeting. Melanie, now a fitness trainer and women's empowerment leader, smiled as Wynton turned the talk to an evocation of her anatomy, continuing a monologue that was also a satire of so-called street talk. Their lasting affection for one another was palpable and the happiness of the brief occasion stayed with me long afterwards, the way you remember a song you first heard long ago.

Now, back in Boston, as the van pulled into the side entrance of the Copley Plaza Hotel, where the doormen had their coat collars buttoned and were wearing gloves, I thought about driving home that June night after meeting Sally, raindrops wetting the road, the music fresh in my mind, and I remembered thinking then that it was just three months since my mother had moved to Bronxville from Northampton, where she had settled after my father died. And what, I thought, had Wynton's friend D.J. said to me the last time I visited with him in Los Angeles? D.J. Riley, suffering from a disease called Morquios Syndrome, who spent most of his life now in a kind of bubble, supported by tubes and devices to help him breathe, eat, digest, whose legs long ago had failed him, whose body except for his head had shriveled to half an adult's normal size.

D.J. had first come to a gig when Wynton and Branford were playing at Berkeley many years ago, where D.J. was a law student then. When I met him, he came backstage in his wheelchair. His body was small, and his small legs just dangled there. His head seemed enormous in comparison to the rest of his body. Wynton and D.J. started talking about music and it was very apparent that D.J. knew all sorts of jazz. Coltrane. Miles. Monk. And he knew about lots of other things too. He and Wynton talked about politics and books.

"Hey, man," D.J. would say in his fast musical voice. D.J. talked very fast. "Check this out, Wynton."

And he'd tell Wynton another story. Even then he knew many people; it seemed to Wynton he knew everybody. He got sick sometimes—he had pneumonia one year—but he always recovered and got around again. He traveled all over. Home to New Jersey. And he turned up wherever Wynton was playing in California, he came to all Wynton's California gigs. He'd fly up from LA to San Francisco and a friend would meet him and bring him straight to the gig.

D.J. once called to wish me a happy Father's Day because, he said, in his high-pitched voice, he knew from his own life how important it was to have a father, so he could imagine the feeling of being one. And so, then, on that last Los Angeles reunion D.J. had reminded me that no one ever *knew*, wasn't it *odd* he added that Wynton so hated to fly that he instead drove, or, rather, was driven, everywhere he could, even though being in a car was more dangerous statistically than flying, and therefore *who knew*, Wynton's life could be wiped out in an instant, or he could develop an illness like Muhammad Ali, any of us could, *look at me*, D.J. whispered, *I could walk when I was a kid*.

Like music, like life: experience and memory merged, June and December, rain and snow, Northampton and Los Angeles and Boston, as if I were witness through music to a kind of miracle, participant in my own improvisation, second trumpet in a septet that had only one trumpet (*No, I'm not the manager*, I learned to say when club owners and promoters came up to me, the white guy, wondering if I was the person who should get the band's paycheck, *I play second trumpet*). Walking finally into the lobby of the Copley Plaza, brightly lit by recently restored chandeliers, I bumped into Wess Anderson, *How you doin', Swig, you have plans for dinner?*; pictured D.J. when I first met him more than a decade ago on a mountaintop in Saratoga, California, at the original Paul Masson winery that was now a concert venue, D.J. being pushed then in his wheelchair that starlit night by an Oakland friend of his, Charles Douglas, dead now, and the next day we had seen Charles and D.J. again, backstage, at an outdoor jazz festival in Concord, California, where David Robinson, *Sugar Rob*, after setting up the soundboard in the center of the mammoth covered pavilion danced during the entire gig with his future wife Reni; and listened again in my mind to the voice of a young woman singing near the end of the *All Rise* rehearsal that afternoon in Boston, right after a break during which I had called my mother on my cell phone in the red-carpeted hallway outside the swinging leather doors of Symphony Hall's first balcony, the hall empty and dark except for the brightly lit, crowded stage.

My mother was once a singer herself, a soprano with a clear tone and a striking ability to convey great depth of feeling in the smallest phrase in her favorite repertoire, the songs of Schubert and Ravel. How I wished she could have been with me, I told her on the phone, to hear that triumphant voice in the hall that afternoon singing:

I say All Rise, All Rise, All Rise, All Rise, All Rise, All Rise, and be heard.

And in my mind I had said a prayer for her, which took the form of a song for all my family and friends, for days long past when we lived in the back of a Conway, Massachusetts farmhouse and I used to get up very early in the morning, often to the accompaniment of the milking machine as it was turned on by our landlord, Mr. Harris, and while in the next room Bonnie, pregnant with our first child, slept I would sit by an open window at the dining room table and write another story.

Once, after writing through the night, I heard music from the barn radio early in the morning. I walked outside in the dawn light, where over the sound of the cows and the milking machine the radio brought in a signal first from Nova Scotia and then as the morning wore on Maine and then, finally, the sun shining brightly over the meadow by the brook across the road from the barn, Massachusetts.

"Can I help?" I asked Mr. Harris, stooped over a milk pan, his arms shaking from what might have been the early signs of Parkinson's disease, and without stopping the motion of his hands he looked over a shoulder and answered in a high-pitched, hard-to-hear voice, "When have you ever done any real work in your life?"

He almost sounded like Wynton, years later, upbraiding me or someone in the band for bullshitting. Wynton was particularly critical of what he termed "Negroidal bullshitting," which he defined as promising to do a task and then never even getting started on it. You didn't have to be Black to be accused of being this kind of slacker.

And then, in an instant, Wynton would change the tone, the content, the import of a conversation with a direct question or observation.

"How's our girl?" he asked, meaning Maren.

And he would listen intently to my reply.

"How's your old lady?"

"Where's your son living at? He still in California?"

Some of these questions I answered completely and sometimes I just nodded or replied with only a word or two, or I'd ask similar questions in return.

"What are you working on?" I might say, a question invariably answered with a nod or a shrug, never a word, and then sometimes followed by, "Check this out," and if I were with him he would start playing whatever it was at the piano. On the phone he often did that without provocation, in fact answering the phone he might not even say hello but immediately begin playing part of a new piece, and then he might say, "Hold on," while he took a call on another line, and minutes would pass before he returned, maybe to talk or maybe to play something more, though sometimes he'd forget you were waiting and I would figure out what had happened and hang up.

Wynton never volunteered anything about his extended family or his lady friends. We were talking in the living room of his apartment a few years ago when Wynton, composing at the piano, looked up as I said something about his mother and father when he was very young.

"You must have been very lonely when your father was out playing at clubs," I said. "'Where is Daddy? When is he coming home?' I can imagine you asking your mother. Maybe she even sang you a lullaby. And rocked you in her arms."

"No," Wynton replied sternly. "It wasn't like that. She never sang no lullabies."

He was upset at my perceived presumption. But he didn't contradict me about being lonely.

The next morning he took his sons to the park to play ball, and the day afterwards he left on a fall tour.

I wondered how his sons felt when he left, and another time asked him.

"They know their father is Wynton Marsalis," he replied.

Work was a refuge. If he were about to perform he might pick up his horn rather than say something about himself. For Wynton, the exchange of information that a conversation offered was always secondary to the shared sense of the fleeting, permanent, breathless present that his music affirmed. Though he would listen to another person's problems at length, he kept his own counsel on many of his most personal matters, and he was invariably close-lipped in response to questioning that probed. He would change the subject or just ignore the person who raised it. You had to divine what he meant at such moments and then make judgments, weigh and compare different passing revelations, pickup on an offhand comment, let it drop while he returned to the manuscript of some music he was writing at the piano while you talked, and then later, perhaps, put two and two together.

Two and two;
one-two-three-four;
a one, a two, a one, two, three, four:

Could I write that…what I looked for, what I found…so Maren had to read all of it to understand it?

II
Home and Away

Years ago, during the lengthy period when I was learning to write and taking care, near and from afar, of my dad, for whom the pains of his life were finally more than he could bear, and recognizing the responsibilities of being married, and taking long walks along the South River in Conway and through the fields Mr. Harris hayed and up into the woods behind the farm to the border of the poet Archibald MacLeish's estate and then across through the woods to a mowing hidden high up in the hills (how I would love to show you that magic spot, Maren, there was an old apple orchard near it, too, back when the land was open enough so you could see the whole verdant valley where we lived)...anyway, one of those unborn literary efforts, something I kept coming back to again and again, stayed in my mind as a phrase: *the dance of my friends* was the phrase, which in my mind encapsulated an ambition to circumscribe a collective sense of the lives of certain other people as I understood them, their loves, their losses, all held within a consciousness that first formed itself on summer walks long before, in Vermont, where as a boy I used to hike alone across a meadow whose top looked out in every direction, with the lake we stayed at spread below me, back when our family was still more or less intact, my uncle still living...there was a girl, too, who was more interested in some older guy I of course therefore hated. No one, I thought, knew then what I knew, I mean knew within me what I already was sure that I knew about the grandeur of the world, the seasons, the sky at night, music heard over the lake in the evening, the fragrance of that meadow and the sounds there, crickets and birdsong, the immense expanse of sky. Once or twice, hiking that hilltop meadow, I took my clothes off and walked bare-assed through the field, the hay and juniper scratchy. The dance of my friends mixed in my mind with the wildflowers and pools in the brook years later where I'd stop to spot trout and the paths through the woods that I knew by heart, when we lived so happily at that Conway farm, and there would come these moments when it would all soar, when I thought I could fly.

All my life, Maren, there has been in my mind a sense of these two worlds, that mountaintop and my core, two places, what I will call for the moment the outer and the inner. Trying to resolve the tension between these two worlds has been my private preoccupation for as long as I can remember, going back to my Buffalo childhood when my room was in the rear of the second story of our brown-shingled house, with a window that looked out on the driveway and the neighbor's adjacent yard, and another yard beyond that, lit at night by a hooded lamp suspended from a corner of that family's house about 20 feet above the ground. During the long Buffalo winters, I used to get up in the night and look out my window at the snow, thick flakes falling steadily and quietly. Wondering if there would be enough for school to be called off the next morning, I would watch the flakes falling in the light from that neighbor's lamp. I loved the silence then, our house quiet except for the furnace clicking on every so often. We had no storm windows, and so with the window open a crack some of the snowflakes would blow into the room and land on the sill, where they would quickly melt. I liked to take a little snow on my hand and lick it, trying to imagine where those particular flakes had commenced their brief winter journey...from how high in the winter night sky, formed I supposed somewhere far out on Lake Erie, beyond its forbidding winter shores, windswept I was certain and forlorn, out past the beaches where we swam in the summer, where I was in love with a girl whose family moved to Toledo, Ohio, at the far other end of the lake. Maybe this snowstorm had started there. Who knew? Who ever knew?

We live our daily lives, of course, in the outer world, the world of jobs and family responsibilities and school and mowing the lawn and doing the laundry and going shopping and talking on the phone, all those things that if we are lucky and have our health are a form of grace if you will let yourself think about them that way, be open to them that is, and thankful. And I love that outer world, love the sense of speed driving on the open road or the smell of woods on a walk after rain, the icy chill of the wind on a chairlift in winter. I love the responsive action of the piano keys when my finger tips touch them and the shock of cold metal on my warm lips when I pick up my trumpet and blow through the mouthpiece. I love the pure *sound* of all the instruments on stage or on the bandstand. That isn't music, of course, I mean just those instrumental sounds: the outer world. Not until you're at the other place, *within*, can there be music, which at the beginning of my travels struck me as a paradox. Something had pulled Wynton and still did, compelled him to *go*, even as he had confessed when I asked after we met that he didn't "know" where exactly he was *going*…and so I wondered, what was it, and I wanted myself to "go," to experience, understand…just as I'd read that he, too, at the age of 17, seeing an announcement about tryouts for musical study at Tanglewood had auditioned, been accepted, and *gone*, never come back really, on the road forevermore, so even that year right after Tanglewood at Juilliard in New York City was only another way-stop to…where? And how could I get *there*, too?

But to go back again to the beginning: you were just a baby, Maren, born a few months earlier, when your brother and mom went with me to hear Wynton that first time at the Iron Horse Café in Northampton. So your age parallels the chronology of my friendship with him. You weren't yet two late the following year when Wynton returned to the Horse, continuing to come back to the small, cozy club long after he was so popular that he could have filled a much larger area hall, because he liked the crowded space, with the audience sitting at tables right next to the stage and squeezed onto the stairs to the balcony, and because he remembered that its edgy, imaginative founder, Jordi Herold, had first booked him before he was well known.

At about that time, we'd put our house on the market, the old place on the ridge of a hill that we'd bought after moving from the Harris farm. We'd lived there since just after your brother was born, fixing it up room by room, doing much of the work ourselves and planting a gigantic garden with asparagus and strawberry beds, near the maple by the corner of the huge barn that we'd finally had taken down because it was more than we could handle. But the whole place was; your bedroom at the front corner above the stairs never had heat, in fact the entire second floor was without heat or electricity when we moved in. The outside of the house hadn't been painted in more than 50 years, so the clapboards on the sunny side of the house were not only completely bare but curled from exposure to the weather. We'd replaced them, and fixed the shutters, wired the upstairs and gotten heat in most of the rooms, and downstairs the kitchen had been transformed from a small room with a linoleum floor with pipes that sometimes froze in the winter to a much larger area with new counters and cupboards and a hearth for the stove which burned wood that I split and stacked.

You were too young when we moved to remember it, but I can still see the path in the valley below our hill that we took to the swimming hole and the dirt road up the next hill that your mother liked to hike with our second retriever Molly and the fields across the valley where I went on my cross-country skis after a storm, once with my brother in a deep snow when we had to make tracks and we ended up on the far crest in a clearing where, looking back, I could see our house with its lights sparkling as evening came on and I tried to imagine the lives within it at that moment, my children, my wife, my sister-in-law, my mother who'd come out from Northampton for dinner: human lights.

The first time I returned home from my job and saw the For Sale sign in the front yard, next to the tall maple where we'd hung your sister's tire swing, I stopped my car in the road and stared, then opened the door, got out, and pulled the stakes of the sign from the ground. But I knew we should sell, and the following morning the sign went back in. I was doing some ghostwriting for a businessman just then and office work for a small, early-music outfit with offices near Northampton in an old mill building where the main tenant was an organization that employed the physically disabled and mentally challenged. Seeing some of those people every day made it difficult for me to feel sorry for myself, but I was restless. A book about the Boston Symphony I'd recently published, with the naïve expectation it was going to make me famous, had yet to go into a second printing. Each day at noon I would escape from work into town, walking the gray streets, or to a nearby

9-hole golf course. There, though the golf season was officially over, I hiked the deserted, frozen fairways and hit a ball around the small layout with a 7- or 8-iron. Squeezed between a small, wooded mountain and the four-lane pavement of an interstate highway, the course's location beckoned me to light out for some still undefined territory.

Bundled up on a late autumn day, with the wind blowing near the base of the mountain where the course bordered the woods, I let my thoughts swirl with the oak leaves, always the last to fall, brittle on the ground so they made a crackling sound when you stepped on them. How beautifully their light brown blended with the faded orange and red of the maples. That afternoon I returned to my small, stark office in the old mill building, with its view of a 7-11 across the street and a Mobil station beyond, and late in the day as I watched the sky grow dim and the streetlights come on snow started to fall. By the time I left for the half-hour drive home it was snowing harder, big wind-driven flakes making the sidewalk slippery and the visibility poor. The cold wind felt like a slap on my face, as if someone or something were trying to wake me out of a deep, protracted sleep.

Wynton had left me with a phone number for his road manager that first time we met, the year before, and the next day, still chilly but with the snow gone, I called it. Matt Dillon, "Monyure," answered, and after I reintroduced myself and briefly made small talk about the *Time* Magazine piece I'd recently read and asked about the tour, how was it going—I think they were in Ohio just then, or Ontario—I said I see you're coming to Northampton again soon, and before I was able to say anything more Matt asked, "Do you need tickets?"

And that is actually how my road life began, Maren, with that call, though I was pretty clueless when I made it. I certainly had no expectation that I would eventually visit every state but Idaho and the Dakotas with Wynton, travel to Europe and the Caribbean with him, and spend so much time at Lincoln Center in New York City that as you know it became a kind of second home to me. During one stretch of nearly a year when you were little I was away from you and the rest of our family three weeks at a stretch, then home for a week or so, and then gone again…searching for something, the bridge between my outer and inner worlds, certain I was about to find it at the next gig or town in a chance encounter with a stranger, a surprising conversation with Wynton or someone else in the band, a solitary moment standing to the side of the curtain, backstage, or by the stage door, staring down a quiet street or from a window high in some hotel overlooking the city or the mountains or the sea. By the time you were a teenager I was still on the road, not as often in fact but still in feeling.

As I started to share earlier, Matt had remembered to leave my name on a pass list at the Iron Horse, and afterwards, back at the band's hotel, Wynton invited me to come to Boston the next day. Like my decision to go, the clear, November air on my drive to Boston the following morning was bracing. Though I would be coming home that night, I had an immediate, deep sense of a future that I was determined to reach. Less clear, and at what cost, was the realization that doing so meant I would miss part of your childhood, and your sister's, and the end of your brother's, though in my mind the tradeoff if I can use that word was the expectation that when I was home I would really be *home.* And what times we had, especially when you were little and I rented that office in town after we had moved from Conway to Amherst; you have probably forgotten all the afternoons I would pick you up at school and we'd stop at the bakery and then walk back to my office where you had your own desk by the window that faced the town common, but I remember—your high voice, the way you grabbed my hand when we walked somewhere, the notes you used to write me, with illustrations, and leave on my desk in a homemade envelope, with instructions to read the next morning or, if I were going on another trip, in my plane.

At the benefit concert that night in Boston I listened to the voices around me, to the interplay among the musicians in the band and between them and their entourage and audience as intently as I did to the actual music. Who were these seven men in the band—Wess, who like several others had first played for Wynton when he was still in school; the other saxophonist then, Todd Williams, so serious, with that deep serious sound in his horn; Wycliffe, enormous, and his sound was, too, strong and profound, and how he also let loose with his voice sometimes; Herlin the drummer, New Orleans born, father of five, not counting his dead sister's kids, took care of them too, steady, rock solid; bassist Reginald Veal, Swing Doom everyone called him, also from New Orleans, married at that time to Kim who joined him whenever she could on the road, she worked for Delta Airlines and so could fly for free if she weren't working, *oh I'm going to see my baby tonight*, Reginald would sing when he knew she was coming; and pianist Eric Reed, a preacher's son, irreverent about life in the band and religious about the spirituality of his sound—what prompted their joy and élan, the depth of good feeling their playing invariably inspired? They were all younger than I, and except for their bus driver, Black. What must they have made of me in my button-down shirt, rep tie, tweed jacket, and Weejans? Certainly if I were going to fit in, it was very clear to me that given the gold standard of couture set by Wynton it would not be on the basis of dress (just about everyone in the band would at some point counsel me on this tricky subject, though the only advice on it that I took completely to heart was Wess Anderson's: "tops and bottoms, Swig," he said, by which he explained to me he meant ties and sox; they were the "key").

Shortly after reaching my destination that first day, as I stood in the lobby of the Park Plaza Hotel where the band was staying in Boston, someone reminded Wynton that they were heading to Maine the next morning.

"Why don't you come along," he said to me. He had just returned from Cambridge, where he'd given a workshop to some elementary school kids and the mayor of that nearby city had presented him with its keys.

"Thank you, but I can't," I said, though there was nothing at that moment that I could imagine wanting to do more. "My oldest is just twelve. I need to plan these things."

And then we were off to join the rest of the septet who were already at the Berklee sound check, and who would remain at Berklee afterwards for a pre-gig supper while Wynton went to get his hair cut before he and I talked at the piano bench after he said goodnight to his kids on the phone.

As we sat together on that bench in his hotel room, I sensed an important moment in my life had come, but I had to find the voice within me to articulate it. I remembered the very first time I played the trumpet in public, at a chapel service for kids; I was about 10 or 11 years old, and my father's assistant organist was going to accompany me in a short prelude my father had arranged for organ and trumpet. I knew my part well, but I was so nervous when it was time to play that my mouth became dry and I could not wet my lips before taking my embouchure. Not a note came out of my trumpet!

"The terror of the trumpet," another musician friend of mine termed this years later. The slightest problem in articulation produced a large mistake in pitch, projection, tone, timbre: all the qualities that, together, made a musical sound. Though by then I had only heard him perform twice, Wynton was the only trumpet player in my experience who seemed not in the least little bit fazed by the possibility, or for that matter probability, that the next train wreck, as many players called it, could occur at any moment. I'd heard a story that Wynton had told about performing Haydn's Trumpet Concerto, back at the beginning of his career when Wynton still played classical music in the concert hall, and after a few bars of the first movement Wynton stopped the conductor and asked him to start the piece again because of a mistake Wynton had made in his entrance. If this were true, it was the only such account I'd come across, and when I'd been around Wynton at the Iron Horse I'd been struck by how calm he was before the gig and between sets. There seemed no separation in his life between being off stage and on.

The same thing was immediately apparent as we sat at the piano in his Boston hotel room, less than an hour before he was to play this benefit at Berklee. We might as well have been in a café somewhere having coffee (or tea, Wynton did not drink coffee—nor at that time alcohol for that matter, though he later developed a fondness for Armagnac after one of his trips to France, in fact the nicest gift you could present him was a bottle of fine Armagnac, which he would imbibe slowly, late at night after a gig, nursing a single glass).

"I want to write something that explains

how a musician goes from there," I said, pointing to his heart, "to here," I continued, placing my hand on the piano keys, and touching with the same hand my own heart, which was beating at what seemed to me its normal rate, my pulse normal, too: no stage fright, no fear. What I said seemed as natural to me as breathing.

Silence in the room, save for the traffic sounds outside by the Boston Common, brightly lit with Christmas decorations. For a second I wondered if perhaps I had said more than I should. It was like one of those places in a piece of music where no one plays a note, everything is suspended, you even hold your breath, and then as suddenly as the music stopped it starts again, but with a different energy and clearer purpose.

"Let's rap," Wynton said, standing. "But I've got to get ready for the gig," he continued.

He was wearing sweat pants and sweater, and it was already past 7:30 p.m. The performance was to begin at eight.

"Talk to me while I get ready," he said, and I followed him into the next room where an ironing board was already set up, and we talked while he pressed his shirt, his suit, and even his tie, and we continued talking in the elevator and out through the lobby to the waiting limo. Once in the car, however, Wynton's focus changed abruptly as he extricated his trumpet mouthpiece from the instrument's leather case that Wes had been carrying for him and played several warm-up exercises on it while kibitzing with the driver about Boston traffic.

The streets of the city passed quietly by, headlights in the window. Wynton laughed at one of Wes's jokes and told a variation of one he said he had just heard in Japan. Sometimes jokes and stories segued so seamlessly that it could be hard to tell which were what.

"I went to this concert at Lincoln Center, heard this young dude, this Russian, playing the piano," Wynton said to me. "He was playing Mozart and Shostakovich.

"I was sitting next to these newspaper critics. They were writing this stuff, it was a strange vibe to see it while this kid was playing the Mozart. I talked to them afterwards, and they were saying, 'Well, the Shostakovich will be his own territory,' you know, all that Russians-can't-play-Mozart bullshit. And I saw this critic, can't remember his name. And he asked me what I thought.

"'You think you could be up there playing Mozart with the Philadelphia Orchestra when you were twenty?' I said. 'I thought the cat was killing.'"

When the Berklee gig ended there was a

reception for benefactors back at the hotel, so Wynton left the hall sooner than he might otherwise have, and I continued to tag along, though it was now late enough that I would be getting home long after midnight. At the reception I made small talk with a few guests and then told Wynton I had to go.

"Let me walk you to the elevator," he said, and despite my protestation that such a gesture was unnecessary he did, leaving the reception for a few minutes.

"How will I get in touch with you?" I asked.

"You'll find me," was Wynton's gnomic reply.

Maren, you were still shy of your second birthday a few weeks after that first Boston visit with him, when I called Wynton on New Year's Eve as he was leaving to perform at the Blue Note in New York.

"When are you coming out on the road with us?" he asked, in a voice so low I could barely hear him.

"Soon," I equivocated, as if this were a summons that would be retracted if I didn't act on it immediately. It was a pointless anxiety, but I did not know that yet, hadn't realized Wynton responded to whatever people were around him at a

Ricochet

given time, betraying little concern about those who weren't, but never forgetting them either. Partly, I supposed, this was how he dealt with a ridiculously crammed schedule, but it was also the outward sign of an inner focus that could be both inspiring and intimidating. In all the years I have known him since, he has never taken an entire day off; never gone to the movies or a show, unless with his sons; maintained a humorous loathing for anything resembling the ocean, a beach, or a pool (when his manager once convinced Wynton to visit Hawaii for a kind of working vacation, Wynton left the day after he arrived); continued on the road to go out to small clubs to play after a regular gig ends, and then be up early the next morning to do a master class; worked steadily and purposefully on *something* every day, despite his procrastination on major projects, staying with his concentration to the very last minute before he has to break for some other obligation (a gig, a rehearsal, a meeting) and then returning to the work immediately upon its completion, alone in his hotel room or at the piano by the corner windows in the living room of his 29th-floor apartment looking out at Lincoln Center and downtown Manhattan and west across the Hudson River to New Jersey, with a sense of the country opening up beyond that western horizon, the country and its towns and cities and all the people he had visited, the memories and energy of which and of whom it was his ambition to put in his music.

That same focus could become an enveloping curiosity about others when they were in his company: no part of another person's life was off limits for discussion with Wynton. He was strikingly open about the physical phenomena, the wonder and elation, of being alive, indeed he reveled in it. He was affectionately demonstrative, touching a shoulder or a head, and often working at home alone in nothing but a pair of boxer shorts, falling asleep in the middle of a conversation or in a hotel, lying on his bed as he talked on the phone.

Once, several years after I started traveling with the band, he was taking a break on the tour bus during the filming of some music videos at Tanglewood, the place in the Berkshires where Wynton studied for a summer after he graduated from high school. He had returned there often to perform and endowed a student scholarship, having himself won the summer of his own residency the award for best brass student, this despite being refused a lesson by one of the Boston orchestra's retired trumpet players, because of his race, Wynton told me (though when I brought the subject up again he declined to say anything further about it, as if he had thought better about saying anything in the first place).

The music videos he filmed with the BSO's music director, Seiji Ozawa, were part of a PBS series for kids. There was an audience of children in the barn building where most of the filming took place, but none in the bus where Wynton had retreated to use the john. It was a hot summer day, and the bus's air conditioner was on while the bus idled under some trees. After using the tiny bus bathroom, which anyone on the road knew by silent decree was for peeing only, he emerged, fastening his belt, and warned whoever was in earshot not enter it for a while.

"Whew!" he exclaimed, smiling broadly. "Nasty."

Wynton entertained band members and close friends while shaving or ironing before a gig—he always pressed his own clothes—often at the last minute, while in the hotel lobby his driver and one of his road managers nervously checked their watches. Even with strangers, Wynton probed the people he was with for information about subjects from the mundane to the sacred. In a single sentence he might go from a joke about farts (for a time he used to extend an index finger in lieu of a handshake, and when the unlucky person grabbed it he would gleefully fart) to a question about the death of a loved one.

"How is your mother?" Wynton asked during that post-Boston, New Year's Eve call before he left to play at the Blue Note. He'd met her the month before at the Iron Horse, where at her request, relayed through me, he had played one of her favorite songs, *For All We Know*, and then acknowledged her by name from the stage, something she never forgot.

"OK, thanks," I said, surprised that someone who was about to perform at a fabled New York City night club could be this laid back, oblivious to the time. "So," I continued, "where are you going next?"

"I have no idea," he replied, which I was beginning to recognize as not only his standard answer to this question but the truth.

A few months after that call I saw him in New York, where he played at Carnegie Hall in an April benefit featuring a host of older, legendary musicians: Dizzy Gillespie, Gerry Mulligan, Freddie Hubbard, all on the same stage. Wynton was comfortable in their company, though he was less than half the age of all but a few of his fellow performers. I think they also included Doc Cheatham, who was in his 80s then, except I may be confusing my memory with a Town Hall gig, also in New York, at which Wynton and Doc played repeated encores to a packed house on a warm, late June night. By the date of that concert I'd already made my first, brief trip with Wynton to his hometown of New Orleans, with a run-out to San Antonio before a return flight from Houston...sorry, Maren, I'm getting ahead of myself again.

After the Carnegie Hall gig I returned to New York often that spring. Once I spent part of a day with Frank Stewart, the photographer, who took me up to Harlem to see an exhibition of collages by Romare Bearden, whose assistant Frank had been near the end of Bearden's life. Frank was married at the time to a strikingly beautiful woman named Helima, who worked at the museum where the collages were on display, and who had been seated next to me at Carnegie Hall. We'd struck up a conversation at intermission, and she'd introduced me to her husband after the gig. Frank and I would become friends—High Point and Swig—but when we met that night there was a mutual, startled moment of wariness and confusion over our respective reasons for being at the gig; we were both, it turned out, planning projects with Wynton. The next time I was in the city Frank invited me to go to the gallery with him, partly, I sensed, as a kind of test.

"There's Black people living there, you know," Frank confided, his eyes sparkling, his manner mock serious.

"I think I can handle that," I said, and Frank seemed pleased by my answer, not so much its content as its tone. We wouldn't see one another again until the summer, when Frank brought his two daughters along on a run-out from the city to a gig on Long Island, and after that not until the following fall, when we found ourselves sitting in adjacent seats on a connecting flight from Chicago to Lincoln, Nebraska, where the septet was beginning a tour that took us also to Kansas, St. Louis, Kentucky, and Louisiana, and during breakfast in a downtown Lincoln hotel on a very cold, winter-like day Frank explained the foundation of his view of Wynton's musical world.

"He is the sun," Frank said, taking me aback.

Frank, who'd grown up in Chicago and studied photograph at Pratt, was a street-wise intellectual who did not make wild claims. He was also pretty unflappable, one of the reasons Wynton eventually asked him to assist as a driver several years later when after a near-disaster on a plane Wynton decided to avoid flying whenever possible, even if that decision meant as it often did a lengthy van or car ride. Talking, Frank might crack a slight smile to let on when he was kidding about something, but he was dead serious about his work, and his photographs had an edge to them, a depth, making them at once a document of a particular moment and an insight into a meaning or evocation of a feeling. Frank's photographs—of musicians, of Bearden, of everyday folk—weren't so much "about" their subject as they actually "were" the thing they depicted: the essence of an experience, whether musical or romantic or political.

The afternoon of the Bearden exhibit was gray and chilly, and I was cold walking from the subway station to my next stop, Lincoln Center. Wynton had started to perform there in a summer series called Classical Jazz that would soon develop into a program called Jazz at Lincoln Center, of which Wynton would become the artistic director. Jazz at Lincoln Center would in a few years boast of its equal status with the New York Philharmonic, the Metropolitan Opera, and the New York City Ballet as a full-fledged Lincoln Center constituent, and yet in stark contrast to those other organizations, which would become engaged in squabbling over Lincoln Center finances and renovations, Jazz at Lincoln Center would one day move into its own headquarters in the huge new Time Warner building at Columbus Circle, where Wynton and his bands started playing in performance spaces that cost well over 100 million dollars, much of the money personally raised by Wynton, who charmed donors with an irresistible combination of humor, self-deprecation, idealism, and chutzpah.

Wynton did have a way of creating attention, negative or positive, despite his constant disavowals of seeking publicity. To judge from what had been written about him Wynton was not only the "enigmatic," "visionary," "charismatic" heir to an entire artistic tradition, an iconic standard bearer, but also, according to some observers, close-minded, interested in only one kind of jazz, and thus…a polarizer.

"Why is it," he would ask rhetorically, "that someone else finds it so threatening when a Black man has something to say *and* says it *and*—this is truly crazy—can also *play*?

"I don't know why these people call me," he continued, referring to an interview he'd just done.

"Did you see the piece in the *Voice*?" I might ask.

"What did it say?" he would reply.

But he knew.

One of my closest friends, a screenwriter who'd moved in his early 40s from Hollywood to Israel, grilled me soon after I went on the road about an incident he'd heard of second-hand that falsely questioned, he said, Wynton's partiality. Later, after my friend had been diagnosed with a rare form of lymphoma, he left his hospital room one day in California to meet me at a workshop Wynton was giving in a West Oakland housing project.

Working with kids seemed in some respects not so much a byproduct of Wynton's relentless touring but one of its primary purposes, as if Wynton were on a kind of mission if not to save the world with jazz at least to make jazz a more important part of its future. Some of the claims he made could come across as grandiloquent, and far removed from the wellsprings of an art form that began in smoky night clubs and old-time dance joints, but few who listened to him in person could resist responding to his importunings and cajolings. He had a way of being heard, not just with his music but with his words.

Geographically, the housing project where the Oakland workshop took place was only a short distance from a neighboring community called Emeryville, where at a club called Kimberly East, I once sat in for Wynton at a rehearsal, an experience that helped me realize, as Wynton cheerfully pointed out to me later, when he heard reports of my difficulties, that I was not a trumpet player (I could not keep up with the sheer velocity of the music with my eye, let alone my lip). Instead of the boutiques and restaurants of Emeryville, here in West Oakland the most prominent landmark was the collapsed expanse of Martin Luther King Jr. Boulevard, badly damaged in the 1989 California earthquake.

Workshop in West Oakland was also something of a misnomer. None of the kids in this gathering seemed musical, or particularly interested in music for that matter. They were all attending a summer program designed to improve their scholastic skills and, at the same time, feed them if they were hungry and take care of them if, as seemed to be the case for many, no one was at home to do so. We were staying in the tony San Jose suburb of Los Gatos, where the septet was performing that night at a mountaintop winery. Voluntarily participating with him in that Oakland workshop was trombonist Wycliffe Gordon, who had grown up in Augusta, Georgia, and whom the other members of the septet had taken to calling Pine Cone, or just Cone for short, because the nickname expressed something about his personality and background, the country aspect of an outlook that was mixed so explosively with musical wizardry (he could play half a dozen different instruments well) and a style of improvising that was both technically sophisticated and intuitive.

Before the workshop, which lasted about an hour, I introduced Wynton to my friend, whose illness I had mentioned to Wynton on the long ride over from Los Gatos that morning. Sitting in the back seat of a limousine, working on the score for the *Citi Movement* ballet commission he was months late completing, Wynton had looked up, held his pencil in mid-air, and we exchanged rapid-fire questions and answers about my friend:

—Why was he in a Berkeley hospital if he lived in Israel?

—Because this is where his Boston-based doctor had recommended, and it was relatively near his wife's family in Sacramento.

—What was the prognosis?

—Much better now, but still uncertain; he could have died.

And then, without further comment, Wynton had returned to his manuscript, despite his agitated distress that day over the news, delivered to him in person in his hotel room the night before, that his tenor saxophonist, Todd Williams, had decided to leave the band, for reasons having to do with his religion and being away from home so much.

"How am I ever going to replace Todd?" Wynton asked rhetorically as we waited for our host outside the building where the workshop was to take place. That's when my friend showed up.

"Wynton, this is…." I began.

"I know," he interrupted me, and then, in

the same breath but to my friend, "How you doing, man? Thanks for checking us out today. But tell me something, please"—and he nodded in my direction as he finished his question—"how could you be knowing this man all these years without going crazy over all his bull"—brief pause, drawing out the vowel before the double consonant—"shitting?" Then, quickly following, came loud laughter, a smile, and a hand on my charmed friend's shoulder.

Afterwards, still at the housing project, Wynton spied an outdoor basketball game and asked if he could play. Right off he tried a few outside shots, his specialty, and missed. Driving to the hoop, he reversed the ball as he dribbled behind his back and made the layup. He clapped his hands and bounced on the balls of his feet as he ran for his position on the next play. Again, he missed a jumper from foul-line distance.

On the other side of the court, a young man about 15 or 16 edged toward the basketball players, oblivious to their proximity. The look on his face was vacant. He was wearing two pairs of pants, one over the other. The outer pair had suspenders, which were undone. This pair of pants had fallen down to his ankles, making it almost impossible for him to move. But he did not reach down to pull them up. Instead he had slowed his

Ricochet

walk to a shuffle, even as he moved into the midst of Wynton and the other basketball players, who continued their game and tried to ignore him.

On the ground at one end of the court, near some little kids who were hitting a volleyball, lay a dead pigeon. No one apparently knew how it had gotten there, or why it had not been taken away. But as Wynton retrieved the basketball from out of bounds, he watched as the man wearing two pairs of pants shuffled toward the pigeon, stopped, bent over, and picked it up. Holding the pigeon in his hands, the man then resumed his shuffle.

Those nearest the man stood back, giving him all the room they thought necessary; they'd seen this behavior before. The man appeared to be going toward a loudspeaker from which was booming hip-hop, but changed his mind before he got there. He headed back toward the area on the other side of the basketball court, where a little grass was growing in the space before the buildings. A few small trees had been planted in the courtyard, too.

Driving back to Los Gatos later I made what I immediately realized was a gratuitous comment on the plight of this man and the bleakness of where he lived.

"That's an opinion," Wynton shot back,

looking up from the music he was again working on. He was visibly engrossed in this process, but betrayed none of the excitement he felt when he had finished something, like the afternoon several years later before the premiere of *Blood on the Fields*, when he was talking with several friends who had gathered in his sons' bedroom, and as he bounced a basketball on the apartment floor said, "I really got to something here."

Back in the car from West Oakland to Los Gatos, Wynton continued, "My mother grew up in a housing project. Never judge. You never know."

By the time of that conversation, my evolving career as second trumpet had been consecrated with Wynton's agreement to collaborate on a book with me. During a springtime visit to New York we had made a presentation before a dozen or so people gathered around a table in a conference room at the offices of one of New York's largest trade publishers. Though we had not prepared for this meeting, our impromptu give and take provided me with my first chance to practice improvisation, albeit verbal rather than musical, with Wynton. When Wynton replied to a question about Duke Ellington's memoir, *Music is My Mistress*, I added a comment about his answer, even though I hadn't read that book, and we were soon inventing the dialogue format we eventually used for our book. There would be many more chances to practice in New York, where Wynton often entertained guests after a gig with improvised, usually profane lyrics he called the Hoghead Blues (accompanying himself on the piano as he sang, except one time backstage at Tanglewood when he was waiting to perform with pianist Marcus Roberts and the two of them serenaded an amused Seiji Ozawa with a lyric about an imaginary girlfriend of Seiji's who'd supposedly left him), or on the road.

After our presentation we had gone out to a celebratory lunch at which Wynton made such prolonged eye contact with our literary agent that she had finally looked up from her food and asked Wynton if he wasn't going to eat his. Was it okay, what he had ordered, or was he not really hungry?

"It gives me greater pleasure to watch you enjoying yours," Wynton had replied, in the first and only exchange I remember his having with this woman.

A few days later I drove down to New York again for a Lincoln Center gig at which he was making a solo classical appearance. An older musician friend of Wynton's was present at the gig, a white-haired man who had known Wynton at least since his single year at Juilliard and who called him not completely in jest, Mozart, a nickname

Wynton said was disrespectful of Mozart but that over the years I would hear others use, including his longtime producer when he was with Sony Classical, Steve Epstein, a man who by temperament and training was not given to hyperbole.

"Just tell what really happened," Wynton would say to me in response to such excessive praise. Labels, whether positive or negative, avoided imaginative engagement with the subject, which required a different kind of thought and observation. Now that I reflect on it, Maren, the distinction he had in mind was a little like what I called outer and inner, don't you think? I mean, the analogy may break down but what else could he have been referring to as we talked about our book in his Alice Tully Hall dressing room after that guest appearance and I mentioned that his search for a new pianist to replace Marcus Roberts, who had recently left the septet to start a solo career, was the kind of event that could set in motion a good…magazine story.

It was a shame, Wynton continued, that in all the commentary about such musicians as Duke Ellington and Miles Davis, there was really no documentation about something as basic as "what it was like to be in a room with one of them.

"What they left for me, what Duke left, and Trane," he continued. "When something is great, it echoes, and each echo is bigger than what it came from. Think of the sound of a bagpipe in a battle. Or go to the edge of a canyon and shout, *HELLO!* The major function of your existence is to do something that will ricochet, like the echo of your voice from that cliff."

My own impressions of what it was like to be in a Northampton or Boston or Oakland room with Wynton were at such a variance from what I had read that I eventually came to wonder if people who wrote about jazz believed it was someone's opinion of music, and not the music itself, that ultimately mattered—especially this music, sprung from a history of heartbreak and violence, prejudice and hatred, created by a people whose ancestors were brought to the United States in chains in the galleys of ships, this music that nevertheless celebrated life and affirmed the intrinsic individuality of each person and, how could this be, the collective goodness of humanity.

Wynton himself would remind me many times about his heritage. How often in my travels, commenting to him about his lack of sleep or some kink in his schedule had he replied: "I could be picking cotton." Or we might be in a car together, going to a gig, and his mood animated he would start in with the driver, like he had in a limousine on the way back from another gig many years later, when he announced he was really a black Dick Cheney planning a war for oil in Africa and the driver started laughing so hard—Wynton had observed that in the car there were two Black men, a white man, and an Indian-American woman, "perfect criteria to apply for a grant"—that I thought we were going to crash.

In New York that night after the Lincoln Center gig our conversation continued outside after the Mozart-calling friend had left. It was a nice night, warm enough that you didn't need a jacket. Wynton was headed home, which was a brownstone in the Village that was either for sale or had already been sold; he was moving out, soon to be living in a condominium on a new building adjacent to Juilliard (where, with the addition of space from the adjacent condo, he still lives, as I write—the place you've visited, Maren, and where Anna stayed overnight one Christmas, when we'd seen Wynton at a Boston gig where he was playing as a sideman to help out drummer Ali Jackson, and when he, Wynton, learned that Anna was flying out to California from New York very early the morning after Christmas, and we didn't know how we were going to get her to the airport, said, "she can stay at my place the night before, one of Herlin's sons will be there and two of mine, and I'll have a car pick her up for the ride to the airport").

"Let's walk," Wynton said, starting purposefully, and without waiting for a reply from me, down Broadway. He ignored something I said about his performance, seemed not to hear my question about Mozart, and started telling me about his sons, who were one and three years old at that time. He had witnessed both births, he told me, and then described the scene of those miracles, his word.

"This will be my ninth New York City move," he said, but when I asked him for details, such as the actual date or how his sons felt (they were going to be living with their mother, eventually outside the city in Westchester), he clammed up, except to confess the difficulty he had dealing with the kind of day-to-day details that defined raising a family, "you know, going to the park with the kids for two hours." We kept walking, quite quickly, and gradually the rhythm of that walk helped set a rhythm for our conversation, and I began to feel more at ease, less like a visitor and more like someone on a walk.

We passed the Sheraton, near Carnegie Hall, and I mentioned staying there when I'd come down to the city with the Boston Symphony Orchestra for a performance of Mahler's Second Symphony. Wynton did not have anything to say just then about Mahler, whose music I gathered he had played in a youth orchestra in New Orleans, though we would later hear the BSO in Mahler Three at a concert that Wynton would leave, after the first movement, to take his sons who were with him back home to his apartment, where he put them to bed before returning to Carnegie Hall on time for the symphony's climactic finale. I asked him about Mahler Two as we walked, but he had a way of changing the subject by simply going, "uh-huh," if he thought he was being interviewed, instead of having a conversation, and he took the talk elsewhere.

"My grandfather used to run a segregated hotel," he said. "In New Orleans. This was before Civil Rights, when my mama had to sit on the back of the bus. I can remember sitting back there with her."

Not wanting to interrupt the feeling of his memory, and thinking about what had just happened when I brought up the subject of Mahler, I didn't press him with more questions. We kept walking, and the reminiscence resumed.

"The hotel closed after integration," Wynton said. I could not tell if he was wistful about the end of that period in his family history or encouraged by the change in society it represented. Many times when he said something there was no value judgment implied or to be made; it was just a statement of fact.

"Fact is," he would say.

"Yes?" I responded quizzically.

"Take a flower pot, someone's favorite flower pot," he continued. "The wind blows it off its stand and it breaks into many pieces. What happened?"

Before I could reply he answered his own question.

"The flower pot broke," he said. "But that is all. If the person whose favorite flower pot said it was too bad, what happened, that is not a fact but a feeling. A feeling is not a fact. A fact just is."

Fact is.

He had another word for that, too.

Isness.

Wynton's grandfather ran a segregated hotel: *fact*.

It's revealing that Wynton's grandfather ran a segregated hotel: *feeling*.

Wynton is moving out, his sons are going to live just with their mother: *fact*.

That's too bad, that Wynton won't see his sons as much anymore: *feeling*.

We were making our way downtown. As we neared Wynton's street, 18th, we passed an outdoor basketball court.

"Yo, fawly!" Wynton hollered to someone

shooting baskets.

"Play here whenever I can," Wynton continued, making me wonder if we were going to stop and do so now. But we continued to his brownstone, which was locked, the lights out, everyone asleep.

We went into the kitchen, where Candy had left a note saying there was some cold chicken in the refrigerator.

"You hungry?" Wynton asked me.

"I'm okay," I replied. "I had something earlier."

"So, where you staying tonight?" he said as he stood in front of the opened refrigerator door and ate a piece of the chicken.

"I was going to take the train to my brother's. He lives north of Yonkers."

"What time is the train?"

"I don't know, I think the last one is at one, or maybe two."

Wynton looked in the direction of the mantle, where there once must have been a clock but now, with most of the stuff already packed for the upcoming move, the only item on the mantle was a miniature statue of Louis Armstrong.

"Why don't you just stay here," he said, more as a statement than a question. "I'll get you some sheets and a towel."

I followed him down some stairs to a closet, where he rummaged around for the linens he had promised, which he then handed to me and said, without any further conversation, "Good night."

By my next visit to New York, Wynton had completed his move to the apartment by Lincoln Center. Some days the boys were with him, Wynton Jr. (who also went by his father's nickname, Skain) and his little brother Simeon. They had toys that they keep at the apartment, and extra clothes.

"We go out someplace to eat and then we hang out," Wynton said. "I give them a bath, together. We make it a long bath. I mean, when I give them a bath they get *clean*. Shampoo. Everything." The boys both slept in Wynton's bed with their father, the three of them together. His bedroom then, before the apartment was expanded, was off the hallway, separate from the living room around the corner and the little kitchen and the other, smaller bedroom where he had his books and that became a study when an extra bedroom was added for the boys as they got older. Wynton's CDs were in the bedroom, and there was usually one playing; Wynton would leave it on, too, when he went out. After he gave the boys their baths and read them stories he returned to his piano to work until long after midnight. Friends often came by, young musicians who were in town or studying next door at Juilliard, people he'd met on the road whom he'd invited to call him when they were in New York, lady friends.

Wynton dressed the boys in the morning, once in matching outfits, even the caps matched. Then they'd take a few toys and ride the elevator downstairs. Simeon liked to push the buttons. Sometimes they'd go out for breakfast, and they might get a cab if it was a day when no one was picking Wynton up for a meeting or recording session, and they would drive downtown where they still lived with their mother.

"There's the old house," Wynton Jr. once said as they passed the last street where they all lived together. It wasn't much further to Candy's. They'd get off at the corner.

Wynton Jr. might run ahead and ring the bell, and Candy might already be outside with him when Wynton and Simeon caught up.

Candy would greet Wynton, who said little in reply. He might tell her what the boys had eaten, who had a sniffles or whatever. Then they would all go inside, where Candy began fixing them breakfast.

"What a fateful day that was, in Brooklyn, at that restaurant, when we met," Wynton said to me one day on another walk. "Once, before we broke up, we were thinking about moving to the Crescent City so my boys could grow up there, I could see them whenever I came back to the city."

No such reality in his life now. They had sold the townhouse where they'd lived, with the statue of Pops that Wynton still had, and that courtyard where the boys had their stuff. Their first Thanksgiving after splitting they traveled to Candy's family's home in Washington.

At gigs in New York Candy would bring the boys. "If I can't see them from the stage I can hear them," Wynton liked to say. "Then I can see them because the people around them get upset and I can see those people moving in their seats. Squirming. 'Who are these boys making all this noise at this concert I paid all this money for?' My Daddy always took me and Branford to gigs when we were young. And we'd be sitting just like Skain and Simeon, wondering why we had to be there. But you got to take them. You never know when one day they are going to hear something."

As I fell asleep that night after our first long walk, I could hear his voice and Candy's from down the hallway, but the house was quiet in the morning when I awoke, and no one stirred as I let myself out, still wearing my clothes from the day before, and took the subway up to Grand Central where I got the train to my brother's and retrieved my car. I did not see Wynton again until June, which is when he actually played that gig with Doc Cheatham (I checked!), but I called him once in May, after we'd received a formal offer from the same publisher we'd visited together that April day we adlibbed our plan for a book, an offer that meant with its promise of an advance that I could finally afford to join Wynton and his band on the road.

He was in Japan the day I called him, and with my miscalculation of the time difference I managed to wake him in his hotel room with the ringing of the phone. But he took the call, which he kept short, and he mostly listened without asking questions to my news. And then, thanking me for calling and admitting he was a little sleepy, he added three words before hanging up: "Great days ahead."

O'Hare Airport, Chicago

Dear Family,

It's almost nine a.m., Central time, and I just arrived in Chicago (where it's sixteen degrees outside). The flight from Hartford was smooth, and we went right over Buffalo. I could see the Peace Bridge. It looked like one of those bridges at a toy store. And the mist from Niagara Falls looked like smoke coming out of our electric train engine. I had a cholesterol-rich doughnut at the Hartford airport, so I skipped breakfast on the plane and slept after reading the newspaper. We came into Chicago from the north, but I was snoozing before remembering I could have seen Wrigley Field. Now I'm waiting at the gate for the flight to Lincoln. Wynton and Frank are due in from New York in a few minutes, and we're sitting a row apart on the Lincoln flight, which is supposed to take about 90 minutes (we leave at nine-thirty). After checking into the Cornhusker Hotel we have a sound check at three and the gig is at seven, I think. We leave for Kansas City early tomorrow morning.

I love you all very much and miss you very much. Take care of each other and be happy. Hope you get some sleep, Maren and Bonnie.

Maren, you've probably figured out that was a note I sent from the road, soon after my travels began. It gives me a funny feeling to read it now, I mean to imagine exactly what I was thinking when I wrote it, and what was happening in all of your lives. I'm also struck by the semblance of a chronology it begins to lay out, like all my notebooks but different, too, because of its intention. This is more like a document to me, a kind of "proof" that I did whatever I did, but what I'm describing seems in some ways more distant, I mean the time that is evoked is distant. Maybe that's because I was writing more of a long postcard to all of you: *fact*. And it makes me a little sad, within the joy if what I was doing, all these references to things at home I missed: *feeling*.

Mayfair Suites, St. Louis

Dear Family,

It's just after one, and this has been the first stretch of a few hours since I left in that crazy blur on Friday that there hasn't been something to do right away. In other words, we finally got a little sleep on a real bed, after an all-night trip from Kansas City (actually three-thirty a.m. to just after noon Monday), which was followed at three by a rehearsal in the hotel's restaurant and then dinner last night for the whole band and a lot of other people at Todd Williams' parents' house. In another hour now, we go to the hall here (the same hall the orchestra uses) for a sound check that will also be recorded, so Garth Fagan will have more of the music for the ballet (he's choreographing it as the band learns it, the process made more difficult by the fact that the copyist who was writing out parts last month in New York, when the score was being faxed each day from Europe, made so many mistakes that we have another copyist named Ronnie Carbo with us who is virtually redoing all the parts as Wynton corrects them).

I'm eager for news about all of you. Christian,

hockey results? Anna, how was Sunday's rehearsal? Maren, tomorrow morning we're going to Kentucky!

B., I still don't know my arrival time Tuesday in Hartford. Also, could you send any good mail care of the Meridian, if you can mail it conveniently now, or otherwise fax me anything nice. The Meridian is the New Orleans hotel where we'll be by Sunday. Or you can reach me right here, tonight. Thank you!

St. Louis is in old, large city that has the look of Chicago but not the feel in the streets. I walked yesterday down to the Mississippi, just to get a little exercise, and saw the arch, which is kind of hokey, I think, but amazing nonetheless, that it stands. And the ballpark is nearby. The hotel we're in your grandfather would've loved; lots of old wood paneling in the bar and restaurant, and elevators that are still hand operated, and chandeliers hanging everywhere. What's missing is all of you, whom I love very much, and think about always, and talk about, too—Maren, I told Todd Williams about your toy saxophone, and Christian, the photographer Frank Stewart has a daughter almost your age, and Anna, Garth Fagan is the same Garth Fagan you saw at Jacob's Pillow.

Much love, Dad/Carl

Bowling Green, KY

Dear Family,
We're just arriving in Bowling Green, after an

all-morning drive from St. Louis of about 300 miles. We've been eating chocolate chip cookies that someone gave Wynton, a shoebox-ful; he doesn't like that kind, so there were more for us. Yesterday, after the rehearsal for New York City, Wynton, Wycliffe, and Wess went to a high school in East St. Louis, where the band director is a friend of Wynton's. We stayed almost three hours, with the guys sitting in with the kids in their band. I was supposed to go out later that evening with Wynton to visit a friend of his who collects records, but we had our signals crossed and I got some sleep instead; now, as soon as we reach the hotel, Wynton has a workshop at Bowling Green University (I think it's called), then a sound check at three that will be recorded to send to Garth Fagan, and then tonight the concert is at eight, I think. Tomorrow we leave pretty early for Tennessee.

    It's fall here; the landscape looks a lot like home. We crossed the Ohio River a while ago; it's about the width of the Connecticut but deeper. The weather's warmer now than yesterday in St. Louis when the temperature was in the 60s. I walked by the ballpark, where I could see in by the bleachers. Workman were installing the new carpet in the outfield. There was a sign outside that said: Cardinals-Mets April 6.

    I want some news! Send a note to the hotel here, give me some hockey scores, the weather report.

Anna, I hope your cold is getting better and no one else gets it. When I called yesterday, Christian, sorry I missed you. What fun it was to hear your voice, Maren!

We just pulled into the parking lot. Nothing like where we just were; a highway strip with pizza place next door, etc. I love you all and miss you and think of you with each place we pass, which brings me closer to when I will see you all again.

Bowling Green

Yo, Tintin,

It was great to hear from you! And everyone in the band loved your drawing. Was that me or Wynton?! Actually, I was playing his horn last night after the concert here (in an old movie theater). Earlier, he led a workshop for some college and high school students who were nervous playing with him but it all worked out. Wynton talked with them about some of the things you're learning on the piano, like those chord progressions, and he also answered questions about practicing and other things. He said he used to practice four to five hours a day when he was a kid, and when someone asked him what his "first break" he said it was all that practicing, "which is still giving me my break."

Right now we just had breakfast at a Howard Johnson's and are about to bus it to the Smoky

Mountains in Tennessee, where it is supposed to be very beautiful. Congratulations on your team's first victory! Good luck tonight against the Caps. Give my love to everyone, and I hope Anna is feeling better and can skate tomorrow. Isn't today that surprise party of her friend's?

I wish you all were here right now. My window looks out on courtyard and indoor swimming pool in which I wish I were watching you swimming. Also, there is a pool table and a putting green. I wish you could see our bus, which has purple trim on the outside and small letters on the back that say, "Star Trax Celebrity Coach."

Lafayette, Louisiana

Dear Family Whom I Will See Soon,

I'm writing this in a conference room at the hotel. We've been out all day at workshops (three of them), after a drive yesterday through the bayou from New Orleans (and we had crayfish for lunch, pronounced crawfish), then a rehearsal at the hall, concert, recording session until midnight, party at a local politician's fancy house with outdoor hot tub (it was raining, though), then tomorrow we leave for the last stop, Shreveport, which is up towards Oklahoma. Lots of gumbo, not much sleep. The concert Monday in New Orleans was actually something of a letdown, not well promoted and many empty seats, but I did get a chance to see a little more of the city, and saw Wynton's father Ellis again when we stopped at his house on the way to the concert hall at Tulane so Wynton could leave off his laundry!

I loved getting your letter, Anna, before we left New Orleans. Let's see, if this is Wednesday you must have been at gymnastics. Any new tricks? I imagine there must be hockey game soon; Brattleboro Sunday? I'll be there!

Shreveport, Louisiana

Dear A., B., C., and M.--

It's a lovely day in Louisiana, sunny and warm, most of all nice because tomorrow at this time I will be counting the hours rather than days (or weeks) until I see you. This has been a good trip, but I missed you all very much. Will you remember me?!

Morgans Hotel, NYC

Dear Family,

It's nine-thirty and we're about to walk over to the recording studio, near where we were on Friday. I arrived last night after a very long drive, because of holiday traffic, and watched TV while I unpacked and then slept a little restlessly in this very nice hotel, which is also very dark: windows look out on brick, so the shades stay closed, and the lighting in the hallways is subdued (took the elevator down a floor this morning for a free continental breakfast, including fresh squeezed OJ, and all the croissants you could eat, Anna!).

The scheduled today is pretty horrific, with rehearsals this afternoon and evening, but exciting, too. So I will probably not have much free time, or fax time. But I'm thinking of you, wishing you good luck in the hockey tryouts, Christian, and good dancing this afternoon, Anna, and I love you all very much. Maren, are you decorating your room for Christmas?

XXXX, OOOO Dad/Carl

Morgans Hotel

Dear Family,

Are you still iced in? Here it's clear but very cold, and of course I forgot my coat. I'm just on my way to the recording studio for a ten a.m., one-hour session, then a rehearsal at the Brooklyn Academy of Music this afternoon. My sister was planning to come to the premiere but just called to say she has a stomach bug.

Leave tomorrow after meeting with our editor, who is also coming this morning to the recording session. I miss all of you and will see you tomorrow by suppertime.

Wilmington, DE

Dear Bonnie, Christian, Anna, and Maren,

It's about 3:15 and we're in Wilmington, Delaware, after a two-and-one-half hour drive from New York, after last night's Carnegie Hall concert, which was a big audience hit (if you watch on TV, Wynton plays at the beginning, in a piece that was redone after the audience left, and then before and right after intermission, and at the end). My train trip yesterday was uneventful; Maren, thanks for helping me get on the big train. Anna, you must be getting ready for ballet as I write this; and Christian, how was yesterday's hockey?

I'm about to walk across the street for sound check. Not a lot of other news. Oh yes, Bill Cosby came last night. I thought of you, Anna, eating my muffin on the bus this morning--wish I could have figured out send you some—they were homemade. Tomorrow we will we will be in Washington. See you Thursday!

Morgans

Dear Family,

I just returned from breakfast after a very short sleep, because the recording session ended at five a.m. In a few minutes we go downtown for a noontime Christmas program.

It's very cold here, and must be in Amherst, too. Let's get those skis out! Anna, you were terrific in the Nutcracker.

Hope you're all well. I love you very much!

Naples, FL

Dear Family,

It's late, after eleven, and I just got back to my hotel room from tonight's gig, held in a new hall here in "prestigious" Naples. We're staying at the "prestigious" Registry Hotel, a boardwalk to the mangoes by the Gulf where Frank and I went this afternoon, after sound check and dinner (which we ate around four). Trip was smooth, as I reported to Anna. Wynton has the flu we've all had, so he didn't make an appearance until the concert. Naples seems mostly a retirement community for rich white folks. Some medium highrises along the water, but nothing like Miami, and there are long stretches with no building. The water is "cold" (63 degrees), but the outdoor pool, by which I walked on my way to the beach, is 78! There are not the activities we head at Amelia; even the golf course is eleven miles away.

I gather that most of the Northeast is snowed in today; someone on my plane connection from Baltimore said it was already snowing there earlier, presumably the same storm that was heading north. The air here seems to smell of orange blossoms, but I have seen no orange trees, so the fragrance, which I remember from our trip to Amelia, must be something else. Tomorrow we leave early for Kissimmee, which is near

Orlando. I think of our weekend in Vermont, that run we took Sunday morning, Anna, and skiing the bumps with you, Christian, and yesterday's skate, Maren, and I send you all much love this Valentines.

Lexington, Virginia

Dear Family,

It's a chilly gray afternoon in Virginia, where we just arrived around one and are now at sound check at the university down the road from our hotel. I'm going to write this quickly so I can hopefully get it off before Anna's show tonight because, Anna, I want to wish you good luck! I wish I were going to be there to see it in person. Please be sure to order that video for me. And while we're talking about ice, how did you against Greenfield on Thursday, CPV?

Maren, I was so happy that you went to the airport with me. I missed our skating and cuddling. Are you keeping your calendar? I still don't know whether I'm coming home on Monday or Tuesday, but I'll tell you as soon as I know. This morning I was in Baltimore. As we were leaving our hotel to fly down here, I daydreamed about all of you at home on Saturday morning and thought about going out for doughnuts!

Fort Collins, CO

Dear Family,
A quick note to tell you I arrived safely after a

long day of traveling. I was up at 4:30, before my alarm (I was afraid of sleeping through and missing my ride to the airport), and then the man who was to pick me up was late, but we got to the airport with plenty of time. Snow in Cleveland. Sat next to a pilot from there to Denver—lots of stories from an inside perspective about flying. We were at the Denver Airport another two hours, waiting for everyone's flight to come in and locating Reginald's bass, which had been shipped separately. It's now almost 3:30, Mountain time, and we have a 20-minute break before leaving for sound check. It's a funny feeling going through this routine. I know it now so well now, the arrival at the hotel, unpacking, searching for the concert hall. My presence is unremarked upon by the band, and no one changes the subject talking because I am there. Wynton was still quite pleased with his voice disguise a few days ago when he called. Complaining about New York press coverage of Harry Connick this week, called it another excuse for Wynton bashing. Anna, I told everyone about your May visit and they are all looking forward to seeing you!

I miss you all terribly. Be well and remember I love you very much.

Hi, again. This is me, now, I mean not in one of those faxes you were too little to be able to read when I first sent them. By the time of the last couple of notes here I had bought my first laptop and was converting to email as a way of staying in touch, plus of course the phone, though believe it or not there were no cell phones then. So calls were relatively expensive, and email was often iffy.

One thing reading these letters has reminded me of is the tradition you and I established that first winter I was away of going to the skating rink when I was home for a few days, and I'd put you in a chair and push you around the ice as I skated, and then you would stand in your own skates and hold onto the front of the chair's seat and push yourself, maybe with a little help from me. By the end of the skating season, which almost coincided with the end of that long sequence of trips, you could stand up on your skates without the chair and kind of shuffle your feet in a semblance of movement. Now of course you can beat me around the rink skating blindfolded, backwards.

I know you kept asking when that last trip was going to end, because I have a fax I saved that Anna sent me in California, I believe from the time when we stayed overnight in Santa Rosa, just me and Frank and Wynton, before we flew to New Mexico for that weekend when Wynton was finishing the 7/4 section of *In This House, On This Morning*. Anna's fax is of a map she drew of the western United States, and instead of stars showing just the state capitols she has put a star where I was visiting with the band. The star in California also references a note in Anna's cursive (she was almost 9 when she wrote this): *"Where's Daddy?" asked Maren. Here,* the note says, repeating the same word written on the California section of the map, *After California Home!!!*

I neglected to write a date on the back of the map, but I'm pretty sure this was just before Anna went with me to New York for the premiere of *In This House,* still my favorite Wyntonian piece with its synthesis of nearly a century of different jazz styles, all combined with a forward-moving energy that sounds like the feeling of the places we visited, not just New Mexico but all over the country, and the people we met, old, young, white, Black, Hispanic. When we attended that first performance Anna wanted to stay in a "fancy hotel," and so I got a deal through someone associated with the band at a midtown place called the Renaissance. It turned out to be right next to Times Square, which only added to the allure for Anna. We hadn't been in our room five minutes before she had taken all the towels off the rack and arranged them around the sides of the bathroom sink to make an indoor version of the pretend house she used to create among the pine trees that bordered our neighbor's when we lived in the Conway farmhouse. At the concert Anna became restless and spent much of the time with Lesley, an assistant of Wynton's manager who'd come up from Washington, D.C., where the business office was located back then. She rallied afterwards to go with me backstage, where Wynton presented each member of the septet with a watch to commemorate the occasion and thank them for their commitment in rehearsals, learning the piece as he wrote it each day on the bus and in hotels while we were on tour. Wynton spoke for several minutes in that closed dressing room, in a way that reminded me of the private ceremonies that took place whenever someone left the band, except in this case only Wynton spoke.

"We've all made sacrifices to be out here," he said. "You've left your families for weeks at a time. You've stayed after gigs when I called a rehearsal. It's not something that we found when we came out on the road, this life; we had to create it, a group of men working something out. So I just want to tell you all that I love you. Thank you."

The next morning a press conference took place outside, under a tent adjacent to the Metropolitan Opera building, where Wynton and Peter Martins, director of the New York City Ballet, announced plans to collaborate on the ballet that became Six Syncopated Movements, the first collaboration for Wynton with the company made famous by Balanchine, who had worked with such composers as Copland and Stravinsky. And so Anna, whose dancing then would lead to her trapeze work now, was able to meet one of her artistic idols, though as I recall she was—not surprisingly—a little shy when Mr. Martins smiled and offered her his outstretched hand.

Along with that map Anna made me there is a poster she designed that, unrolled, depicts in a sequence of scenes an imagined version of my travels, as well as a few notes from her that I saved. I'm guessing these notes were written around the same time as when she made the map. Her notes were always decorated with artwork, too.

In one of her notes, framed with what appear to be the stems of a purple flower, are the words, *Welcome Home Daddy!* This note unfolds, like a card, and there is another message inside, without artwork.

> *To: Daddy.*
> *We missed you!*
> *We're so glad your back!*

III
Blues for My Father

For almost a year after my father's death, we didn't have his piano tuned. The man who had owned this piano played the *Art of the Fugue* by memory. It was my son who seemed comfortable hitting its keys, and his curiosity led naturally to a search for a local piano teacher, with whom he began studying at the age of seven; his sisters followed in turn, with Maren the last to start...and quit.

The piano books my son used when he was first taking piano lessons were illustrated with four-color caricatures of monsters and clowns and eighth-notes with faces and fingers. At his teacher's request, instead of dropping him off at her house I used to take a seat in the room adjacent to the one that functioned as her studio. I rarely said anything as he learned chord inversions, played a piece we had practiced at home during the week (would he remember the pedal in the coda?), and fidgeted as his teacher explained the week's assignment—understanding the minor mode or the difference between a note marked staccato and a slur that ended with a staccato. He was a good pupil, and for a time he worked harder at the piano than I ever did; later he learned a little jazz piano, too, before becoming obsessed with recorded techno.

During his lesson, I occasionally stared out the window at the maples in the yard, which bordered the road and a brook beyond. Eventually the sound of my son's playing became associated in my mind with the vision of afternoon light in the leaves.

We usually stopped for a snack afterwards, or I rewarded him with a pack of bubble-gum cards.

"Gary Carter!" he shouted.

I loved the way his voice rose at such moments. We talked about the Mets, his favorite team in those days (though his favorite player was a Yankee—Reggie Jackson, whose name for a time he substituted for his). We discussed his playing and the new pieces he had to learn. Sometimes I practiced with him, sitting in a chair by the piano bench, and I frequently used sports analogies to explain how he should concentrate before he began playing or how he should approach what his teacher had assigned.

"Think of that fingering like you were getting ready to bunt," I would say. Or, repeating advice my father had given me, "Get the rhythm right."

My own lessons ended when I was 13. My final repertoire consisted of two works, a Bach prelude and the Adagio of Beethoven's *Pathétique* Sonata. I was also studying the trumpet then, and sometimes I broke the monotony of my warm-up by humming part of the Beethoven. The warm-up consisted of slurred intervals that sounded in my head to a repeated sequence of vowel sounds, "Ouu, eee, ahh, eee, ouu." Relaxing my lips as I moistened them before beginning a breath, I wondered at my decision to quit the piano. Then I remembered that learning Beethoven had been no different. Music was work.

Less taxing were the mornings at home when I was very young, and the radio station that played classical music was turned on in my parents' bedroom. The programming always ended with the chorale theme from the final movement of Brahms' First Symphony, so that when I hear that piece now I immediately think of my mother making the beds. At night, my father came home while I was playing Schmidt exercises or John Thompson little pieces. He took the pipe out of his mouth before walking over to the piano to pat my shoulder. I wished I were outside, throwing a baseball. If my father were a lawyer or a doctor, I could tell him now how much I hated to practice.

Stubbornly, I stuck with the trumpet until college, when I realized my high register was never going to be firm and clear without many more hours of practice. And my triple tonguing wasn't sharp ("Tu-ke-tee, tu-ke-tee…").

My childhood trumpet teacher's studio was located above a store that sold pianos, electronic organs, and television sets, and I was watching the World Series on a floor model there, after a lesson, when Bill Mazeroski hit the home run that beat the Yankees in 1960. That was the year I played Grieg's *Wedding Day at Troldhagen* at my June piano recital. I used to get nervous on such public occasions. Though he could be very stern when I was practicing ("that's a G in the left hand," my father might yell from the kitchen, as I played the piano before dinner), he was kind when I made a mistake in a performance. He wrote pieces for me, and we went to concerts together as a family, when it always seemed that the skies vied with bare tree trunks and branches for the title of peerless gray (it was a draw), reminding me that on this Sunday afternoon in November when the days were getting shorter and inside the music hall my brother and I were enduring another session of a musical indoctrination, our friends were at the Buffalo Bills football game.

*

We never knew, beforehand, what pieces of music were to be played at those concerts; it was quite enough to hear the performance when the time came. The initial agony of it all--two, two and an half hours of cultural imprisonment, interrupted only at intermission by a Coke in the basement lounge, mercilessly not over until the last person had left the hall and our father had congratulated the soloist, spoken with the stage-door manager, and told us, finally, to button the coats we'd been waiting in from the moment the applause had stopped and the house lights had come up. For a long time the only other relief in that childhood routine was the quest for another autograph of an artist whose work we had listened to while playing tic-tac-toe on the program or the anticipation, always rewarded, of hard candy the timpanist would proffer when we visited him onstage, after the concert, as he was covering his kettle drums with pieces of canvas cloth colored a muted beige, suggestive of, but hardly synonymous with, the brass splendor of the drums' outer shell that the cloth covered.

Like many of his fellow players, the timpanist—a short man who sported an immaculate brush of a moustache and spoke in a high voice that belied the stern visage with which, during a piece, his squinting eyes watched the conductor for his cue—was a friend of the family. Sometimes, waiting out the minutes until we could go home, I thought it seemed my parents knew everyone. That was neither true nor possible--the hall sat a few thousand, the orchestra included over a hundred--but they did know more people who worked in or for the orchestra or attended the concerts than I saw at school during the two-week intervals between concerts.

We knew the old man with a cane behind whose house we parked our car. We knew the women who sold tickets, whom my father always spoke to, though we had season seats and didn't need to wait in line at a window. We were greeted by name by the white-haired gentleman who took tickets at the door we always entered, unless we had come in backstage that day; I envied him because I supposed, by virtue of his employment, he was excused from the duty of actually listening to the concerts. We knew, too, the women in muted dresses who handed out programs and showed patrons to their seats. We didn't need their guidance, of course, but, when I'd become separated from my parents before the start of a concert while they conversed with another friend, I occasionally indulged in the ritual of presenting my ticket stub to one of them and being ushered to "my" seat (really a lounge chair almost, with a thick cushion and a fuzzy back, and not at all conducive to attentive appreciation of the music, but when I was very young I was more interested in counting the recessed light bulbs in the ceiling or trying, in the darkness, to read the ads in the program after the first piece had begun).

Attending concerts, we were told, was a privilege. Music was a joy, its makers artists, its listeners lovers. I could understand, in a vague way, why the musicians showed up: they were, after all, being paid (though not enough, my father would say). But all those others, in the audience--women in their finery, their husbands in three-piece suits, students in the balcony: who were they? why did they come? what subtle coercion prompted an action which was disguised so cleverly as to appear voluntary?

The timpanist liked to tell jokes. Sucking on a butterscotch lozenge or a peppermint life-saver which he'd just given each of us, my brother and I would listen to him share a riddle, the delight of which, though we didn't realize that then, was the way he immediately gave the answer, between sucks on a piece of candy, always in that high voice, and with a smile that seemed to say, "I understand what you're going through." Unlike the other musicians (or the audience, for that matter), he didn't have to sit during a piece; he could even walk around a bit. Whenever he played his drums, the success or failure of a particular passage hinged partially on his ability to come in at the right time; I suppose this was just as true, in a way, of a second violinist, but the timpanist was all by himself.

The pressure, I eventually grasped, must have been enormous. Hadn't I heard, from my father, the story about the drummer who lost his job because of the mistakes he made during Ravel's *Bolero* when the great Toscanini was conducting? Yet our timpanist was cheerful, suave, modest, and self-demurring. He would rather tell jokes afterwards. During a piece his hands moved sometimes with lightning speed. Bent over, he would cock an ear to each tight-skinned kettle to make sure it was properly tuned; in a minute, when the sound he had unleashed was supposed to cease, he would muffle it with a quick, hands-down gesture, all the while watching the conductor and keeping count.

"Here, look what I've got," he would say afterwards, as he reached into a pocket and produced a licorice, a mint, or one of those fruit candies with the soft insides, the kind I didn't like though I could never tell him and would wait until later to spit it out.

"The melody is not the song," Wynton will often

say, and perhaps his listening sessions with Branford when they were growing up were preparation for that insight. Even now, when he is trying out a singer or instrumentalist, Wynton will ask a musician to play the bass part or sing, say, the alto harmony, just as, during a perhaps partly apocryphal high school moment when Wynton and Branford were listening to a Bach chorale and Wynton asked Branford, "What was that note just then in the tenor part?"

"E flat," replied Branford offhandedly.

Then they stopped the recording and checked the precise place in the music. And the note was, in fact, E flat.

"How'd you know?" said Wynton.

"It had to be," replied Branford.

When I first heard Wynton tell this story, I was reminded again of my own childhood, when I would be practicing on one of the two grand pianos in what was the largest room in my family's house. Playing the piano was not a choice; it was simply something you did, like eating and sleeping, and when after graduating from eighth grade I exercised my choice to opt-out, as it were, my parents correctly predicted this was a decision I would regret all my adult life.

But when I was young the piano could feel like torture, especially when I made a mistake that was corrected by my father, in the nearby kitchen, where he was talking about his day with my mother as she prepared dinner.

"That's a G in the left hand," he might say in a loud voice.

It had to be.

By that time in my life my father had given up his position as artistic manager of the orchestra to devote himself to teaching and to playing the instrument he loved, the pipe organ. Serving as choirmaster and organist at one of the city's largest, most prosperous churches enabled him to perform every Sunday and practice throughout the rest of the week. Nothing gave him greater pleasure than to be at the console of the magnificent Aeolian-Skinner organ he had designed, with its twin pipe chambers, facing one another from each side of the rear balcony that served as the choir loft, and with a division of trumpet-sounding pipes on the wall between and an antiphonal register of other pipes hidden at the opposite end of the church, behind the nave.

As a boy, I often kept my father company on his early Sunday morning walk from our house to church, and then I would sit by him on the organ bench as he reviewed a last time the music for that day's service. He would nod when I was to turn a page, but he said very little other than a brief hello to choir members as they arrived and a reminder to me to help myself to the licorice drops he always kept on one side of the console, below the array of knobs and switches that activated the different combinations of pipes.

I did not understand this then, but my father was teaching me something I only began to grasp when I was much older. The lessons were ongoing, continuing at the Sunday afternoon concerts of the orchestra, on whose board my father remained, and whose music director was my godfather, the Austrian conductor Josef Krips.

"Shush," the orchestra's personnel manager, Gene Bishop, would say, as I entered Josef's dressing room during a concert intermission. "The maestro's changing his shirt."

Once a member of John Phillips Sousa's band, Mr. Bishop was also my trumpet teacher. The man who had to impose discipline backstage, making certain all the players were on time, he must have been the gentlest person who ever guarded the door of a conductor's dressing room. Balding, he had a thick, wide moustache and enormous brown eyes, which looked even larger behind his silver, wire-rimmed glasses, and his eyebrows, which were the same gray color as his moustache, were as expressive as the multiple furrows of his forehead whenever he smiled, which was often, or placed an index ginger to his lips to signal quiet.

Mr. Bishop smoked Camels, and a tiny piece of tobacco or cigarette paper was often visible on his moist, upper lip. That was his "money" lip, the one that had enabled him to have a long trumpet career, and that must have impressed the man whom an entire country used to refer to as the March King. He didn't play often by the time I was studying with him—only during an occasional Wagner prelude or one of the Mahler symphonies or during the last movement of the Sibelius Second Symphony.

I remember exactly where I was sitting the day I heard that piece for the first time. I had moved from our customary place deep in the center rear of the hall to a spot midway toward the front, on the right side, in an empty seat next to that of a friend from school whom I had arranged to meet. Looking straight ahead, I was in line with the trumpets, who sat in the rear of the orchestra, stage left. Then, on a trip to New York City, I had bought an LP recording by Eugene Ormandy and the Philadelphia Orchestra of Respighi's *Pines of Rome*, which my father thought might "broaden my outlook." But it was that Sunday afternoon concert concluding with Sibelius's Second Symphony that I first heard something that stayed with me afterward. Josef was conducting, and so of course I went backstage to see him during intermission.

" Ah, my Carl," was Josef's greeting as he fastened his cuff links while studying the score for the next piece he was conducting.

I have his autographs from those visits, dozens of them, and a baton he gave me, with a cork handle, which had broken in half during a concert. And I have a book about him, a tome weighing more than a pound, which arrived several years after his death in a brown package with an Austrian return address. As soon as I saw the cover photograph and title I knew his third wife Harrietta must have sent it to me, because she had corresponded with my father when she started it. There, beaming at the musicians in one of the last concerts he conducted, was the radiant, expressive face of the man who after he left Buffalo had been the conductor and music director of the San Francisco Symphony.

When Josef had first arrived from Vienna in 1954 to be the music director of the Buffalo Philharmonic, my father and he struck up a friendship, both personal and musical, which eventually led to annual Good Friday performances of Haydn's *Seven Last Words* at my father's church. I spoke to Josef after one of those services, too, as though it were another concert; what a forbidding look he'd given me when he sensed I hadn't been properly moved by the religious aspect of the occasion.

It was the closeness of my father's relationship with Josef that led to the christening one cold Thanksgiving morning of me and my siblings with Josef and his second wife, Mitzi, as our godparents. Thereafter, every Thanksgiving, we each received a check, deposited into our savings account. My first such check came with a handwritten note:

Love your parents. Love music. Love your country.

Josef—and he always preferred that we call him just Josef—used to arrive with Mitzi each fall for the symphonic season, and the drive to the airport became an annual event for our family. Later we would visit him in the hotel apartment where he and Mitzi always stayed and watch in awe while he drew off almost an entire filtered cigarette with one enormous inhale, then drink a whole glass of beer in one huge swallow.

His musical appetites were grand as well, though they tended to fall into distinct and fairly conservative categories. Josef looked upon almost any twentieth-century composer as being modern, and his tastes were decidedly traditional, with a particular love for Mozart and Beethoven. Mozart was a god, the closest friend a musician could have, a guide to all that was beautiful in life. One of Josef's last recording projects for Phillips was the complete Mozart symphonies with the Concertgebouw Orchestra.

After Josef recorded the five Beethoven piano concertos with Artur Rubinstein as soloist, my father arranged for Josef and Rubenstein to listen to tapes of those recording sessions in the parish hall of our church while Rubenstein was in Buffalo for an appearance with the Philharmonic. The two men sat for an entire Saturday afternoon, listening to their recorded performances, nodding to one another over an especially fine moment and smoking enormous cigars.

Occasionally, I would tag along with my father to a rehearsal. And I loved being with him behind the scenes at concerts, parading through the auditorium after the lights had dimmed and everyone in the audience had taken their seats. When I became old enough to do this myself, it felt natural to me, a habit that I have never lost.

During one of the earliest meetings between Josef and my father that I remember best, the soloist for that week's concerts was also present. Something had not gone right in that morning's rehearsal, and so the soloist had been summoned to meet with the maestro. I believe the piece was the first piano concerto of Brahms, and if I can trust my repeated response hearing it years later, it was a passage near the end of the second movement when a ground bass adds tremendous tension to a sequence of descending chords the pianist plays. What I recall with great certainty is the image of my godfather sitting next to the soloist at the piano in the living room of his hotel suite, the two of them lost deeply in the score, which lay before them above the keyboard because it was too large to rest, upright, on the piano's built-in music stand. Rapidly turning the pages, Josef would suddenly stop at a place he had apparently marked and ask the soloist to play his part.

"Yes!" Josef would interrupt in a voice that was by turns impatient or passionate. And then, as if words could not fully explain what he was after, Josef would sing the phrase in question, all the while gracefully moving his arms, as if he were on the podium conducting. Music, I was never to forget, was a human activity of the greatest import, truly a matter of life and death.

What must have been going through Josef's mind that afternoon in his hotel suite as he led the humbled soloist through what I am sure must have been a trying experience for them both? What did Josef *hear*? From what events and encounters and experience did his sense of the sound he was looking for originate? What was it that he *felt*, that he understood the composer felt and somehow, through the performance, would if things worked out as they should be felt by the people in the audience at the next performance? The concerto came into its final form after the death of Robert Schumann, and Brahms may have composed the second movement out of both his grief over that loss and his love for Schumann's widow, Clara, a pianist. What encapsulation of the world as Brahms had experienced it could be found again in the music these two men were making here in this dimly lit room in a brick building at the corner of Delaware and North in the city of Buffalo, New York, what sleight of musical hand, what transforming miracle of art, what willed, brave, human achievement?

I last saw Josef a few years before his death, when he conducted the Boston Symphony Orchestra at Tanglewood. As a young man, my father had been a member in 1940 of Tanglewood's first summer conducting class, whose most illustrious graduate was Leonard Bernstein. We came regularly for concerts when I was a boy, sometimes renting a cottage in the Berkshires, and we were always present when Josef appeared as a guest conductor. When Josef's 1969 Tanglewood appearance was announced, I was living in Providence, Rhode Island, just a few hours away, and had only recently been married.

For what turned out to be his final Tanglewood performance Josef had chosen to close with Schubert's "Unfinished" Symphony. As his guests, my wife and I were seated in a box with Harrietta. Now, more than half my lifetime later, I remember few details of the performance, but I distinctly recall that upon its conclusion I walked backstage with my wife to greet my godfather, just as I had during those countless Sunday afternoons as a boy.

I had not seen him since he left Buffalo. He looked older, even a little frail, but my sense of being with him was otherwise unchanged. He embraced me and made a big fuss about meeting my wife. In response to questions, I spoke briefly about my early writing efforts and mentioned that we had seen his Buffalo predecessor, William Steinberg, conduct the BSO in Providence.

I knew better than to stay long in Josef's dressing room that summer Sunday afternoon. There was nothing I could say about the Schubert performance that Josef did not already know. Before we left, he asked about my father, whom he addressed with a form of endearment that no one else I knew of ever used: "Hansie."

Usually my father had one month for vacation, but

one summer we spent two months in the Adirondacks in an old boarding house that we rented with my father's brother's family. The house was a big clapboard Victorian, with a porch that went around three sides and a double-decker porch in front. Downhill and through the woods was Lake Pleasant, and the nearest town was called Pleasantville.

We left Buffalo soon after the last Sunday in June. Our Plymouth station wagon was packed full, and I remember that my brother and I made little "forts" in the luggage space. We took the Thruway, exiting at Utica, and arrived an hour later in Pleasantville before our cousins, who also brought a teenage babysitter named Ottie with them. My father's brother was working then for *Colliers* Magazine and only came on weekends except for one two-week stretch.

The bedrooms were on the second floor. The center one in the front opened onto an extension of the porch and looked out on the lake. That was my bedroom. There wasn't much in it--a brass bed, dresser, musty wallpaper. One night that summer I was reading in bed and a bat flew into the room. My father and uncle came to my rescue, using brooms to chase the bat away while I hid under the covers.

Downstairs was a large living room and an

even larger kitchen. We used to play cards in the living room on rainy days and at night. I remember a sun porch on the west side of the house with a hammock. That was where I stepped on the ukulele that had belonged to my grandfather. I was afraid that I had done irreparable damage, but my uncle was able to get a violin maker in New York to glue it back together. At a party the weekend after my uncle returned, the grownups stayed up late playing poker. There was an old piano in the house, and my father accompanied my uncle on the repaired ukulele. Everyone sang old songs and the house echoed with their voices.

For some reason we didn't swim directly below the house but instead would drive a mile or so to a beach shielded by pine trees that gave off a strong scent on hot days. We'd change behind some bushes before walking into shallow water with a sandy bottom. Once I was caught spying on a guest as she changed into her bathing suit. Shame! We built great sandcastles. I remember a warm afternoon when Ottie the babysitter offered to help me on one and I refused. She was very upset and cried. My aunt had a talk with me and I apologized to Ottie, but I felt guilty about it the rest of the long summer.

One rainy day in the Adirondacks my father helped us make a scale to weigh the stones we were selling in our pretend store in the carriage barn across the driveway from the house, near the meadow where the apple trees grew. Another day, I hiked with him through the meadow and he showed me how to stick an apple on the pointed end of a birch sapling and pull the birch bark back, with the apple still on the end, then let go and watch the apple fly across the meadow toward the house.

There were tears when we left. Returning to Buffalo, I remember how the city seemed strangely foreign, with the late August breeze blowing the leaves in the elm trees along Richmond Avenue. But it was exciting getting back for the end of the Bisons' baseball season. Even going back to school was interesting for a few weeks. Seeing my friends, riding my bike, playing catch with my best friend down the street, wiffle ball in the back yard with my brother. Our parents seemed glad to resume routines.

But there must have been nights when my parents thought back. My uncle was healthy then. My father was well established in his work but not so entrenched yet that there weren't still new things each year. It must have been around then my mother began leading the freshmen glee club at the private girls school where my father had become the one-person music department since resigning his position at the orchestra, or maybe she started a year or two later when my sister went to school. Money was a concern, if not an anxiety, but there was apparently enough to live on.

We never went back to the Adirondacks as a family. Indistinct and blurred not only by the passage of time but because I was only nine then, those two months are mixed in my memory with the recollection of other summers. In my mind I hear imagined calls for dinner, requests to do a small chore, invitations to play poker (my father was an expert who enjoyed teaching others) or catch or go swimming or to town or walk back to the apple trees to shoot apples. I smell the pine trees by the beach and the meadow in the afternoon by the hammock on the porch. I hear the rain on the roof late at night when we kids had gone to bed and I'd finished reading and downstairs I could hear the voices of my parents and aunt and uncle and whoever was visiting (from among a constant stream of guests), playing cards or singing or just talking or perhaps sitting on the porch in rocking chairs, listening to the rain or the crickets and thinking about how their children were all asleep and healthy and maybe we'd all go to the double feature in Pleasantville tomorrow. I touch the grass outside in the front and see the paint peeling on the porch and feel wet sand in my hands. I see the white house as you'd see it from the road, much larger than it actually appeared years later when my wife and I went back to look, and though there were trees by the drive as we went up to the house, what I see most clearly is the sun on the south side in the afternoon, making the green grass look almost yellow and lighting up the porch with shadows cast in long, strong shapes from the pillars and railing: the incredible ease with which all those phantom shapes move inside and outside with time to spend--two months!--time that seemed so long then, an entire summer, together, nine years before my uncle died and never again, wherever we were or however happy for other reasons, did you speak innocently in our family about the past.

The sailboat race will begin in a few minutes. It is a sunny weekend afternoon, the last in July, and I am standing on a raft in the center of Caspian Lake in northern Vermont. In one hand, I hold a flag that signals the boats to approach an invisible starting line extending from the raft to a nearby buoy; in my other hand, I am clutching a stopwatch, my index finger on the button that starts and stops its ticking...

...Four years after the Adirondacks, our family began spending the month of July in a rented house on a lake in Vermont. For my father, our vacations there were everything his childhood summers in New York had not been. Other than his work each morning at a lawn table by the lake, there was no sign of ambition in my father's summer activities. He liked talking with people at Willy's General Store and at church suppers, and he was excited when he caught a glimpse of one of the community's famous summer people, who included the author, John Gunther, and, it was rumored, Greta Garbo.

"She bathes nude every morning in the lake," Dad said he had been told.

He took great pleasure--greater, I'm sure, than my mother, for whom it meant extra cooking and an intrusion in her routine--in welcoming overnight guests from home. They included a couple from our church who were on their honeymoon. The bride, whom my father had known since she was a girl in his junior choir, was a "knockout"--his word, which he used with delight. Her husband, a lawyer, drove a Corvette, which made him an idol in the eyes of my brother and me. Another visitor was a young musician, one of my father's best organ pupils. How my father loved telling the story afterwards about the night they all went skinny dipping and this man had insisted on wearing his bathing suit.

"So I asked him, 'What do you think you

have to hide?,'" my father said. "And he answered, 'The body is a temple.'"

Laughter brought tears to my father's eyes, and my mother had to beg him to stop. Wearing a short-sleeved shirt with an Hawaiian print and baggy Bermudas, he carefully filled his pipe with Dutch Amphora, lit it, and clenched it in his teeth so that his lips formed an almost perfectly horizontal line. Then his eyes widened and he grabbed the pipe from his mouth as the laughter began all over again...

...I know well many of the places I can see on the distant shore. At one end of the lake is a public beach, behind which a short, dirt road leads to the center of Greensboro, which is little more than a built-up four corners, with a gas station and the store facing each other across a small common. A path, beginning at the beach, circles the lake along the shore; it is the route we take when we travel to town by foot...

...Though we shopped regularly at Willy's our major grocery trips were to the larger town of Hardwick, several miles to the south. Prices were lower, and there were separate hardware, clothing, and liquor stores. Hardwick was located in a valley, hidden from our view as we drove toward the town until we came to a crest in the highway and saw below us the tops of trees and a white steeple. The Idle Hour movie theater, where we went for weekend nights, stood out on Main Street, and a local soda-pop, Barr's Better Beverages, was bottled in the town. We bought it by the case.

Our rented house, with its fieldstone fireplace and wicker furniture, its small kitchen and smaller, second-floor bedroom, was empty most of the day. Only at night or when it rained did we spend much time there. In wet weather we played Monopoly and poker or we read, unless we took a trip--to Craftsbury Common, where my parents shopped for antiques, or to St. Johnsbury, where there was a coin-operated laundry. On Sunday nights there was always a concert of classical, recorded music, played over speakers from the porch of a house about halfway between ours and the public beach. People went out in their boats or canoes and, on the lake, listened to Rachmaninoff and Brahms...

...I cannot see our house, hidden behind pines, nor can I see the dirt driveway extending a quarter mile to the road where our mailbox is. Not far from the mailbox, another, smaller road starts past an old farm and rises toward a brush-covered mountain pasture...

...We bought our Sunday newspaper at the gas station in Greensboro, which was always a busy place, because the owner was also the town's main real estate agent. Crossing the road to Willy's, we waved to passersby, most of whom we didn't know. The store smelled of sawdust, sprinkled on the floor behind the butcher's counter. There was a penny candy counter near the cash register, where long strips of red and black licorice competed for attention with Tootsie Roll Pops and miniature Mars Bars.

Up the road from the store, past a series of white frame houses with large porches and larger lawns, a golf course had been laid out on a former cow pastures and named for its mountain view. Until just a few years before, the greens had been roped off to prevent cows from eating the grass. The holes alternated uphill and down, and along the fifth fairway there was an old well with a rusted pump, still working. From where we lived, it was a two-mile drive to the course where my brother and I rarely broke 50 for nine holes. Though he was always happy to drive my brother and me over to the course and pay our greens fees, our father never joined us for golf. He did come to our Little League games though. He was too awkward at sports to help with the coaching, as some of the other fathers did, but he more than made up for this with his enthusiastic cheering…

…The climb is steep, and I have to stop occasionally to catch my breath. I hike with the lake, a mile away, behind me, and only at the summit do I turn and remember…

...My brother and I were among several summer out-of-towners who played on the Little League team. We practiced on a hayfield and played games against teams from nearby towns, including cheese-famous Cabot, where each July fourth there was a fair. Cabot had a real baseball diamond, with a backstop and outfield fence, and the stands were filled for the game. The starting center fielder, I'd never played in front of so many people. I made several errors that day and have never forgotten the feeling of helplessness as ball after ball fell out of my glove. On one line drive, I tried to redeem myself by making a shoestring catch and ended up trapping the ball in my glove on one bounce. There was a runner on third who broke for the plate, and I came up throwing. The ball sailed straight home, about 20 feet too high, and cleared the catcher, the umpire, and backstop.

Our coach was a medical student from New York City. Why didn't someone good enough to coach want to be a major leaguer? I had a long talk with him about it, at my parents' suggestion, and I asked him--this was after the Cabot game--if he thought I'd hurt my chances of making the Yankees. He said there were other things in life besides baseball. Shagging flies one warm evening during practice, the smell of clover and the sound of crickets in the air, I wondered if he knew what he was talking about.

Roger Maris was chasing Babe Ruth's record for home runs that year, and I used to walk up the driveway to the mailbox every morning to get the *Buffalo Evening News*, which was mailed to us from home. I'd turn immediately to the sports section and check the box that compared Ruth's 1927 statistics with the progress of Maris and Mantle, who had a good chance at the record, too. A friend who lived on our Buffalo street sent me clippings from *The Sporting News*, and I'd sit in the hammock on the porch and study them, while my mother made the beds and swept the floors and my father worked at the small table he'd placed on the shaded lawn between the porch steps and the water's edge.

Our second or third summer in Vermont, my uncle rented a house there, too, and that was the last time both families were all together. My uncle's height was no longer imposing but awkward; his ribs stuck out in a bathing suit and, after exercising, his breathing was labored. He had started to get the shakes. Our house came with a rowboat, and he liked to go out in it with his young son; my uncle rowed, the muscles in his back bulging, and we watched them at twilight from the shore...

...*The boats have made their big turn and are*

moving towards me now. Red and yellow and blue nylon sails blend with the off-white of canvas, and all across the lake are whitecaps. A wave crests, and I put my free hand in the warm water and let it dangle there. Feeling the rocking rhythm of the raft, I look up at myself as I look down. Then silence, save the wind in the grass and the ticking of the watch.

The last time I saw my uncle, deep furrows marked the hollows under his bloodshot eyes. His breath smelled of nicotine. His handshake was firm, but his hands twitched when they were not occupied. Flakes of dandruff were scattered on the shoulders of his suit-coat. The skin around his chin and cheeks seemed stretched, so that the bones stood out, while his shirt collar fit loosely around the tendons in his neck. He spoke in a quiet, slow voice, sometimes not completing his sentences. Keeping his eyes on the road ahead, he did not look at me as he talked. He asked simple questions about my father and the rest of the family, and how was I doing in school. He said nothing about himself or the circumstances under which we had met at his home in a New Jersey suburb.

Having the day before attended a conference for high school yearbook editors at Columbia University, I had taken the bus from Manhattan to visit my cousins, whom, I discovered, my uncle was also visiting; he lived now in a hotel in New York and saw his family only on Sunday afternoons. I accepted his offer of a return ride to the city. Soon we were crossing the George Washington Bridge in a long stream of car lights, which shone in the rear view mirror, so my uncle's figure appeared somewhat in silhouette. He sat well back from the steering wheel, and his long arms looked disconnected from his body. His head nearly touched the ceiling of the car. He lit a Viceroy and took deep gulps of smoke, exhaling with a hiss, his lips barely open. When he stopped the car to let me out, he put a shaking hand on my shoulder and saying, "Give my love to everyone," squeezed until I could feel each finger.

My uncle was two and a half years younger than my father. They had grown up under strict rules, enforced by a father who punished his sons with slaps from a belt strap and solitary hours in a closet. Perhaps it was this shared experience of childhood terror that formed the strong bond between them; or perhaps it was the love of their mother, a stern but saintly woman who according to family legend spent the day before she died baking cookies for a cancer-stricken New Jersey mother whose husband had left her with nothing to support their children. In high school, my uncle had played the violin and been a swimmer--

backstroke champion of New York. Like my father, he did not attend college; there was no money in the family for it, and the Second World War was starting. My uncle commanded a tank in the war and was captured; his family thought he had died. He escaped from a prisoner-of-war camp shortly before the war ended and was sent to the Walter Reed Army Hospital in Washington, D.C.

Once, when I was 12 or 13, on a family visit to New Jersey from Buffalo, my uncle invited me to tag along while he walked the family dog.

"My mom told me you were in a tank in the army," I said as we left the house and headed downhill.

What my mother also told me was that after his release from Walter Reed, when my own father was still overseas, she had met my uncle at the train station when he returned to New York from Washington.

"He was so thin and gaunt I almost did not recognize him," my mother had said, catching her breath as she spoke.

I did not mention this to my uncle as we walked.

"Let's not talk about that," was his cryptic comment to my mention of the war, and he quickly changed the subject to school work. I never asked him about the war again, nor my father, who served as a warrant officer and bandmaster overseas in the army and who, to the day he died, carried in his wallet a photograph he had taken of a victim at the Nazi concentration camp he had helped liberate.

My uncle's career was spent in magazine and newspaper advertising. He did well, and my father spoke proudly of his accomplishments, not, however, without an occasional trace of jealousy over the material rewards that my uncle received and my father did not. My uncle's modern house was located in a small development near the center of a formerly rural town. I remember an evening in April, when we were in New Jersey during school vacation, and my oldest cousin and I walked to the station to meet her father, who took the train home after having crossed the Hudson by ferry. He was wearing a suit, a trench coat slung over one arm, carrying a leather briefcase. He bought us candy in the store across from the station and smoked as we walked along shaded streets past the older houses. He took long strides, and we made a game of jumping to match them.

By then my uncle was exceedingly touchy or overly enthusiastic about the smallest things, but he could still charm with his smile, and it was easy to understand how that natural movement of lips and cheeks had captivated others. He was still a very handsome man. The following fall, he made a so-called business trip to Buffalo and stayed with us. He took my brother and me bowling. As my uncle's health worsened, we were told only that he was sick. My parents each visited him in New York, and my father wrote him every day. He was desperate to help his brother, and that despair began a decline lasting as long as he lived.

In mid-January 1965, a month after my return from the journalism conference, my mother woke me with the news that my uncle had died of a heart attack, alone, in a hospital in New York. He was a few days shy of turning 45. My parents flew immediately to the city; my sister stayed home with friends, while my brother and I followed our parents the next day by train. As we arrived in Grand Central Station late in the afternoon, we could see our father waving to us on the platform with my uncle's two daughters. We greeted one another with hugs and kisses, then, holding hands, walked along the platform to the crowded, main lobby. My father stopped at a newsstand, where he bought the *New York Times*. A loud voice announced the arrival and departure of other trains. Among thousands of strangers, we gathered around my father by the information kiosk in the center of the lobby as he opened the newspaper to the obituary page, which he scanned.

"There," he said to our cousins, pointing to a one-column story near the center of the page. "There, girls, there's your father." Leaning with one hand on my shoulder, hard, he brushed away tears with the other, and we walked from the station without speaking.

After my uncle died, the mere mention of him was enough to plunge my father into renewed grief, and we carefully avoided the subject. Often, when my brother and sister and I were excused from the dinner table, my father would remain, smoking a cigar. Later, he would read on the living-room couch, a tall glass of bourbon and soda at his side, and the smoke from his pipe would rise through the light above the lampshade. He'd get a glazed look on his face and not seem to hear us if we asked him something. He would sit there for several hours at a stretch, getting up only for more bourbon, and sometimes falling asleep on the couch. In the middle of the night, he would wake up and write letters at his desk until dawn. Then he'd go to bed and would just be coming downstairs again as we finished our breakfast before going to school. He'd kiss us goodbye and drink coffee at the kitchen table while my mother washed the dishes, and then he would get dressed and, depending on what day it was, drive either to the school where he taught music or to the church.

*

Our house in Buffalo was set back from the street by a squared section of lawn, bounded on the sides by our neighbor's driveway and our own. Where his driveway bordered our lawn, our neighbor had built a concrete curb, and the man who mowed his lawn mowed also a strip about a yard wide of ours. Our neighbor insisted that the property line was "there, not here"—I can hear him emphasizing "there," unsmiling, as though he might have me arrested for trespassing if I ever forgot, but when I asked my father about it he just shrugged his shoulders. I seemed the only one in our family concerned over the incongruity of our space of crabgrass and dandelions, poorly cut by a heavy, hand-pushed mower, contiguous with the power cut, weedless object of our neighbor's pettiness.

Our reclusive neighbor, a retired businessman whose first name was Frank, lived with his sister. Neither had ever married, and their trips out consisted exclusively of short drives together in their black Cadillac; I never saw either of them so much as walk to the corner drugstore, four houses down the street. Their backyard, separated from ours by a high chain-link fence, was filled with flower beds and rose trellises, which they could see from their dining room window. My brother and I, who had turned our own small yard into a wiffle ball diamond, were often in Frank's yard, retrieving a foul ball, that, because of the risk the retriever ran of angering Frank (he would rap his knuckles on the window and scowl if he caught us) counted as an automatic side out. Sometimes we played pepper with a real baseball, but that practice ended when a ball broke a window in Frank's garage and Frank called our mother on the phone and accused us of having no respect for other people's property.

The window of our second-floor, back bathroom faced the roof of Frank's garage, and one day I made the discovery that, by standing on the tile-capped side of the garage roof (reachable from the top of the chain-link fence), I could touch the window sill. Supporting my weight with one hand on the side of the house, as I leaned across the space between the house and the garage, I managed with my other hand to prop open the window, grab inside, and then pull myself into the bathroom. Beyond the daring of it, this was a momentous event: my brother and I could get into the house without a key. As we grew older, this became a favorite, if not also somewhat dangerous, way to enter, particularly at night, since coming in through the front door meant encountering a dozing parent waiting in the living room or waking one of them inadvertently while walking on floors that creaked especially loudly at late hours.

Several black and white photographs taken by my father in 1949, when he had traveled alone to Buffalo on a house-hunting trip before we left New Jersey, were tucked into an envelope I found after his death. Missing are any shots of the backyard or the window above our future neighbor's garage, but there are two well-preserved prints of the front exterior of our house from different angles, and in one of these, taken from the street, the lawn is dappled, with sunlight coming through the leaves of one of the many elms that used to grow along all the avenues of the city. Not yet is there a curb where the lawn ends, but, instead, the ground slopes gently to Frank's driveway, and the curve of the slope contrasts with the sharp angle of the house's steep roof. The sunlight on the roof is so bright that the entire top of the photograph seems almost to glow, as though in anticipation of the aura of happiness that would surround that house for many years when we first lived there.

"Here you see the driveway," my father had written in black ink on the back of another of the photographs. "Note upper porch is smaller than below, since bathroom takes up part of space. There is the bay window." That is all. There are no people in the photograph, and nothing is said about the interior; perhaps he described that in a letter to my mother that was sent with the photographs. Though this is a point on which the first-time reader might disagree, I detect in the tone of my father's shorthand description more than a hint of the pride I believe acquiring the house gave him. There is also, even in these few words, a style that I recognize immediately as his—direct, personal, and without affectation. We would all, later, learn to distinguish between the positive expression of that personality and the manic joy that was often a mask for the sadness from which he suffered during the last decade of his life; but here, in this glimpse of what I now see as the end of his early adulthood (he had just turned 31), the contentment created by the prospect of a new job in a large, prosperous church, a home on a residential street far from the crowded Manhattan of his childhood, and a growing family—my mother was already pregnant with my brother—that happiness is evoked for me in those five final words: *There is the bay window.*

I did not go back to the house for many years after the hospital across the street bought it, but I understood it had been painted, the backyard paved over into a parking lot, and the rooms turned into neurologists' offices. The thought of an outpatient's being examined in our former dining room was so far removed from my recollection of dinners there that my memory remained undisturbed, and I was able at will to return to our house, to climb quietly the fence by Frank's garage, cross the garage roof, and enter through the bathroom window to look around, pausing at each bedroom to gaze in their sleep at those whose daily lives I once shared…

…The back hallway lamp never works, but I can see my way from the lights through the window coming from the outside lamp over Frank's garage door. I leave my shoes in my bedroom, which is next to the back bathroom, and look down the hallway. It is dark, and the only sound is of my own breathing and, from the opposite end of the hallway, my father's snoring. Never, as a child, did I hear my father describe a dream, and I have difficulty imagining his midnight meditations. There is, of course, the nagging problem of the water pressure; the pipes are too small or too corroded, and whenever someone is using the water in the kitchen a person who has just lathered his hair with shampoo in an upstairs shower suddenly has no hot water to rinse. And the weather forecast is for snow. Half the congregation will probably go skiing and the other half will be unable to get out of their driveways. There may not be enough tenors to do the offertory anthem…

…Standing in my parents' bedroom, at the foot of their bed, my thoughts, too, invariably turned to my Sunday morning walks with my father to church. Our route took us along a street where many of the pillars of the church lived. All the pillars were old and owned large houses. Rarely did we make that walk without my being told that the woman whose new Cadillac was being washed in the driveway by her chauffeur had just learned that she had cancer, or that so-and-so's daughter or son was flunking out of college or the parents were divorcing.

Some mornings the grass on the large lawns would be wet with dew, and the air cool because Buffalo was located by Lake Erie. There might be a heavy mist, too. All the homes on the street had tall windows and solid-looking doors...

...I would be wearing my fire-engine-red sports jacket, charcoal woolen pants, white tab shirt, and crimson tie, and my hair would be slicked back with some of my father's Vaseline hair tonic. There are puddles along the curb with rotten, water-logged leaves that the highway department missed in the fall, and the odor of the leaves mixes with the fragrance of tulips and juniper on the lawn of the bishop's residence, which we have just passed.

We enter the church through the back door, where the kitchen for church suppers is located, pausing for a drink of bottled, spring water dispensed in small paper cups. Then we walk across the carpeted floors of the parish house, which is attached to the sanctuary, and we stop in the church office, where my father shouts, "Good morning, boss," up the stairs to the minister's second-floor study. Sometimes we climb those stairs to the large, book-lined room, the air smoky from the minister's Chesterfields, and he and my father discuss a hymn or a quotation the minister is planning to use in his sermon. Then we retrace our way, picking up several copies of the church bulletin, which my father encloses whenever he writes letters to friends, and we turn at the corner of a hallway and take a few more steps before opening the door to the darkened sanctuary, with sunlight filtered through the huge, stained glass windows that rise almost to the ceiling in a series on either side of the pews. The first thing my father says is, "Baa!," to test the acoustics, as though they might somehow have changed since the day before, which he spent practicing.

Soon, my father is sitting at the organ bench, playing one of the hymns that will be sung during the service. He has already set the register for this and the other music for the morning, and he runs through each verse of each hymn, since the registration varies by verse. At the end of the hymns he plays an amen. He has taken off his suit coat and is practicing in his shirtsleeves. When he comes to the prelude and the postlude, he asks me to turn the pages for him. He has written notes in the margins of the music and over staves, and sometimes I am reading a marking for a fingering when he nods his head, indicating that I've missed my page turn.

Between pieces, he scribbles a note to himself in a margin. Then he begins to play again, the walls of the sanctuary shaking at a crescendo, and this time he whispers, "Now," or "Okay," when I am supposed to turn. Later, after the choir has come, I sit downstairs, below the choir loft, where a deacon is checking the bulletins on the table next to the center door.

At Christmas the church is always decorated with balsam trees that are brought to the church on the Saturday before the Sunday nearest Christmas in a large truck. The church chancel is filled with the balsam trees and the entire sanctuary smells of the sap and the needles. Red ribbons grace the green trees and it is necessary, as at Easter, to hold two services on Christmas Sunday. The first is a shorter version of the second, which is still attended by so many that extra chairs have to be set up behind the last pews and the two doors on either side of the chancel opened so that people sitting in the chapel can hear the service.

When the service begins, I will sit again with my father on the organ bench, where I will see all the heads bow during the prayers. My father's head will not go down; he will be waiting for his cue for the choral amen, his arms raised, eyebrows arched, poised for what seems an eternity. I can hear people in the congregation coughing, I hear the minister say, "In the name of the Father, the Son, and the Holy Ghost," and next to me my father's robes rustle as at last he gives the choir its signal.

Later, I am kneeling at my bedroom window, which I have opened about six inches and through which I can feel the cold air on my face...

...There is snow, too, in the only photograph I have of the house today. Snow covers the front lawn and the roof of the porch, and there are tufts of snow in the shrubbery, now kept neatly trimmed. Whenever I tell people I grew up in Buffalo, they ask about the snow, but they are thinking of quantity and frequency, so I answer only in reference to the sledding in Delaware Park or skating on homemade, backyard rinks (we'd lug the hose out from the basement and water our rink each night).

I say nothing about the penetration of the cold when you walked outside late at night, and the welcome warmth of coming into the house, the lamp on my father's desk left on, the smell in the room of the cigar stub in the ashtray. I say nothing about the winter Sundays when my father cannot find his car keys and we decide again to walk to church despite the temperature, and how deserted the streets are and how quiet, when we enter the church, the old building is.

Nor do I speak about the distant, warm land where my father lived the last years of his life, almost, I think, as if he sensed that by removing himself from our lives—removing his physical presence, that is—he might give us back some of the space his illness had occupied, a space so dense and deep it had by then obliterated first his work, then his home, and finally his family.

Driving back from Boston, where my father had flown from North Carolina for a surgery on a hip he'd injured badly in an automobile accident when he still lived with my mother, we stopped for food at a Friendly's in a shopping plaza just off the highway. Soon after losing his Buffalo church position, he had received an offer from the American Church in Paris, but my mother did not want to go, correctly insisting that they could not afford to live there. An old friend found him a teaching job back in the Berkshires, where he also began playing the organ at the same church in Great Barrington he'd served as choirmaster before the Second World War. Except for brief visits he had not spent time there since that summer when an old girlfriend of his gave us the house where she and her dentist husband lived. We had stayed all that summer, swimming in the Green River and picnicking on Mount Everett, my father with a baseball cap on his head and a corncob pipe in his mouth, grilling steaks in a stone fireplace by a pond off the dirt road that led to the peak. He was terribly unhappy after his return, and when another friend persuaded him to consider moving to Tryon, North Carolina, he had leapt at the prospect.

I pulled the car up to the restaurant and opened the door for him. Handing him his crutch, I held his free arm as he got out, slowly stood, and then gingerly made his way into the lighted building, where we found a booth near the soda fountain. I helped him off with his coat, then returned outside to park. He hadn't opened his menu when I came back in, and I was frightened by his look, which combined deep hurt with anger at the loss of a world he had loved. His first words were a fleeting reassurance.

"What'll it be, old boy?" he said.

We both ordered sundaes.

"Got a light?" I asked, reaching for the cigarettes I'd bought in anxious anticipation of this visit.

"Always have matches," he said. "That was one thing about being in the hospital. I had almost no desire to smoke."

Our waitress brought us glasses of water.

"Sure you don't want a hamburger or something?" my father asked.

I shook my head. His hair was turning gray. His hand shook slightly as he took a drink of his water, and when he put his glass back on the paper mat he spilled a little. In great detail, he described how a piece of plastic was attached to his femur, which had been inserted into a plastic hip socket.

"You wouldn't believe how much it hurt before," he said. The pain was gone now. Eventually, if his recuperation went well, he'd be walking without a limp.

"My doctor says I'll play the organ again," he said. "Even be able to use the pedal. We'll see."

I asked the waitress for some coffee.

"Decaf," my father said, adding to me in a whisper, "Caffeine's no good. Can't sleep."

"How are you, Pop?" I asked, as I reached with my hand for his.

"Sometimes I think I can't stand it anymore," he sighed. "They tell me to take it one day at a time, but that's easy for someone else to say. I don't know what I'm going to do, but I'll manage."

"Of course you will," I said, withdrawing my hand. "You're going to be fine. You'll probably outlive us all, Pop." He was staring toward the large, plate-glass window by the restaurant door.

"I think it's starting to snow," he said. "The driving could be bad."

I excused myself to call my wife. Looking at my father's back, I saw him reach into his pocket and pull out his pipe. He used the end of a spoon to clean the bowl, then tapped it upside down against the ashtray. Again reaching into his pocket, he brought out his tobacco and began to fill the bowl. He needed two matches to get it lit. The smoke from his pipe drifted toward the ceiling.

He was wearing his navy blue sports jacket, which my mother had bought him one Christmas during a family campaign to spruce up his wardrobe. Unlike his impeccably dressed brother, my father had often favored checkered jackets with striped shirts and ties with wild prints. He'd gone along with our attempts to change the way he looked, but the result was somehow the same; he'd sneak in a bright yellow tie or green pants. For a while, his one other concession to vanity in his appearance was his hair, which he let grow longer, before it was the fashion for a man his age. Then he added a goatee. His hair was still on the long side, but his face was clean shaven now; none of his clothes fit well because he'd lost weight in the hospital.

It was snowing hard when my father and I left the restaurant, and the driving was slow. The weather became the focus of our conversation.

"Are you happy?" I asked my father finally. Using his hands, which he placed under his thighs, he shifted his position in the seat.

"I'm happy to be with you."

"That's not what I meant."

"What do you mean?"

He had been alone, late at night, when he'd driven off the road into a telephone pole that had broken in two. After visiting my father at the hospital the next day, I had gone to the auto wrecker's yard to claim my father's belongings, which were still in the car. The windshield was shattered and the steering wheel had been pushed into the crevice of the car seat. Broken glass covered the seat and the floor, and dried blood was splattered on the steering wheel. The glove compartment was open, but nothing had been taken from it. I sorted through gasoline credit cards, the registration, an envelope with the insurance policy in it, some church bulletins, an empty brown bag, a small metal container of aspirin, and a few maps. Under the seat I found a pipe, and on the floor behind the front seat there was a small bag of groceries and my father's briefcase.

"You were lucky not to have been killed," I said to him as we neared our farmhouse.

"Maybe," he replied. "I'd rather not talk about it."

The snow had stopped and stars were shining as we entered my driveway, and I saw my son's face staring out through a kitchen window. He was waving.

"There's your grandson," I said.

"I see him," my father replied. "I've been looking forward to this so much."

I brought the car as close as I could to the back door.

"Well, it's been a long trip," I said, turning to my father. "I hope you're not too tired."

"I'm glad we had this chance to be together," he said. "You were kind to come and get me."

Though he lived another year and a half, I saw my father only once more, in New York. He had composed an anthem for a choir my brother directed, and my father conducted the premiere. Afterwards, we had brunch in my brother's apartment where I gave my father a box of cigars as an early birthday gift. We wrote each other often; he was so upset with one of my letters that he sent it back to me, with marginal numbers added to correspond to his responses, which filled a separate page. After I received his answer, I wrote him another, longer letter, but I was talking to myself. On the phone, he spoke of moving again, when his hip healed—or when my mother joined him, as if the decision she had made not to follow him to North Carolina were somehow going to be changed.

"I'll take a job somewhere, selling tickets at a train station," he said.

"What about your music?" I asked.

"That's over," he replied, my father who at the height of his career had performed Poulenc's organ concerto with the Buffalo Philharmonic at Kleinhans Music Hall, my father who little more than a decade earlier had brought us all back to the Berkshires one summer, where we stayed in the home of one of his old girlfriends from before the war. One day we went to a Boston Symphony Orchestra rehearsal at Tanglewood of Prokofiev's *Romeo and Juliet*, not an open rehearsal but my father was able to get us in because he knew the manager. I see so clearly the swaying of the leafed branches outside the Tanglewood Shed every time I hear that music, see those branches and the memory of my wife's sleeping presence as she lay in the bed we shared that summer off the road to nearby South Egremont and the smile on my father's face as he won another poker hand. And I sense the anxious joy in my mother's heart, joy because we were together—for what turned out to be the last extended time.

How happy she and my father once were, the parties at our Buffalo house, the night the legendary English counter-tenor Alfred Deller sang an old English lullaby to my baby sister, Astrid, as he rocked her in his arms—"lullay, lullay," the refrain went—or the impromptu visits of my dad's

Buffalo friend who owned a plumbing company and drove an MG and smoked Phillip Morrises and carried a sketch pad in a pocket of his hunting jacket and wanted to be a singer and whose wife raced cars, all these people who used to come to our modest, shingled house across from the maternity wing of the Children's Hospital, and they all came because of my father, the spell he cast, his joy, his love of the world and of music and back then of Ruth and always his children and the hundreds of friends, none of whom finally could help him when it became too much for him, living, and how could that be I still wondered, and the question ate into me until more than one time in my life I thought "it" would get to me, too, the dark shadow, which is always there in great music, what Wynton would call the sword, *lullay, lullay.*

The final time we spoke, his voice on the telephone was faint, almost a child's voice in pitch, insistent and plaintive in tone. It was an evening in early August, and we had just finished supper. After years of emergencies during which I had dropped whatever I was doing, I was nervous when I heard the phone ring. Though it was a relief to know it was him, not someone else calling to say he was in the hospital again, I had difficulty assuming my natural speaking voice when I heard his.

"I need to visit," he said.

"When, Pop?" I replied, scribbling a note to my wife who was standing next to me. "When did you want to come?" My wife jotted down the dates of open weekends.

"What's good for you guys?"

"Labor Day weekend. I have a day off and could probably take another."

"That's too far away. I want to come sooner."

I tried to keep my voice calm. Though I knew something was wrong, I did not tell him to come the next day.

"How about two weeks from now?" I asked.

A few days later I was at my desk at the college where I worked, when someone identifying himself as a coroner called and, after the briefest of introductions, told me my father had had a heart attack. My hand shook as I held the receiver, but I was able to reach for a pencil and piece of paper and write down a phone number and the coroner's name. Then, in a gesture I could only have learned from my father, I thanked the coroner for calling. It was a brilliant afternoon, the sky the color of my father's blue eyes and only a whisper of wind in the air.

My brother and I flew south to arrange his cremation and collect his belongings. He had lived in North Carolina for about three years, and, though in addition to his visits he had sent us photographs and letters, I had never seen his last church in Tryon or any of the apartments where he had stayed. What we found when we opened the door to his place forced upon me a painful image of how his life had ended.

The day was hot, and the sounds of the sleepy town outside were barely audible inside those walls. A window by the kitchen table was open, and through the screen came the occasional thump of a car going over a bad spot in the nearby street and the persistent shrilling of cicadas in the yard. An unmade bed stood by an open, curtained window, and boxes of my father's belongings rested in each of the corners of the room, along one wall, and on either side of a desk weighted with papers and photographs and a piano piled with music. The bathroom sink had been knocked to the floor in a fall, and I tried to right it. We cleaned the toilet and the kitchen sink and counters and closed the cupboard doors, leaving condiments and other cooking materials for the next tenant. The food in the refrigerator we threw away. Most of his clothes, which had been stored in a damp basement before he had moved into this apartment, were mildewed, and we discarded them. We left the rest in a closet for the landlord, who said he would find someone who could use them.

In the drawers of his desk were old newspaper clippings, many of them reviews of concerts he had given years ago; letters, recent and old, were mixed with bills and bank statements and prescriptions. A letter to a friend, written in a scrawl and dated the day of his death, lay on the felt top of the desk, and near it I found an envelope, unsealed, in which was a letter to me, written several months before and never mailed.

Hesitantly, I opened it and started reading. Despite all the difficulties that defined the final years of my father's life, I was unprepared for this last message he left me.

To paraphrase, it began, "please let aching dogs lie." At this point, I don't need any preaching. It is a major accomplishment if I can 'crutch' it from one end of the room to the other. I now have my 3d cast—& will have one for at least another 6 weeks. I am in constant pain—have had ulcerations under the cast—& every time I move, it is sandpaper on raw flesh. I spend practically the whole day with the leg elevated—otherwise it swells up (the foot) like a football. I am not seeking sympathy. I could be much worse off. But as the time goes on—it is not better—but worse. There is not an awful lot one can do, lying in bed with your foot elevated. The first thing I think I'll give up is writing—it is hard in bed—and I get little reward.

This may sound like a negative note—& in a way, it is. Why try to disguise? I am jobless (thank God on that one), have no future—at the age where no opportunities are readily available—don't really care.

Heaven only knows when I'll see you guys again. But I plead with you, at the present time, hold off for a little while. I'm in need of the slightest ounce of encouragement to keep going to get thru a day. I'm grateful to have Winky as a companion—while my landlady is in Florida. She is comforting & affectionate (even tho it is a big effort to attend to her needs).

I spend the better time of the days thinking about all of you. Just the thinking is about all I have left. All I'm really trying to get across is that I'm terribly lonely.

A friend gave me a black and white television (and I've learned to live with 1 plate, 1 knife & fork—possessions no longer mean anything to me—even a car—which, at the present time I'm forbidden to drive by my doctor—but which I probably can't afford—so if, & when I can walk again—I think I'll do without a car) (could probably do with a 2nd hand—but that is always risky). I think I'll just resign myself to sitting in my landlady's lovely garden—and keep the waiting game—hoping my turn comes up fast. I've had a rich life—in many ways—the greatest gift is you 'kids.'

I had no idea I could rant on like this. But you

may as well know how I feel. I am pretty much alone—not that that is bad—one's own company is not the worst.

You can send this letter on to your brother—for I'm not up to writing two.

I have bared my soul. I hope I haven't depressed you. I am just being honest. I am so lonely it hurts—coupled with that, I also hurt physically.

You have always been a sympathetic person—and therefore I feel I can write you from the heart.

Love, Pop.

I put the letter back in its envelope and wept.

We scattered his ashes near a mountaintop in his beloved Berkshires a few miles from Tanglewood. It was a place where my father and mother used to go blueberry picking when they were younger and where, as a family, we used to picnic. My father had always loved views, and there was a magnificent one from that spot. His favorite flower, mountain laurel, framed the trail leading to the place where we gathered. Before I opened the plastic bag of white ashes I had carried in a plastic container from North Carolina, we each said a few words and my mother read Psalm 139. Then we held hands and sang a hymn, the music to which an old friend had Xeroxed, someone who had once been a member of the junior choir my father had directed when he first came to the Berkshires before the Second World War.

I was surprised that the ashes weighed as much as they did, surprised too, at the faintly sweet scent they gave off. The day before, in my kitchen at home, I had practiced opening the bag, to be certain I would know how to do it on the mountain. And how could I be sure, I wondered, that these were my father's ashes? Then I had noticed, near the top of the bag, a piece of metal that had not been melted during the cremation. I picked this fragment from the ashes and held in my hand a screw which I slowly realized was a surviving symbol of the hip operation my father had undergone two years before.

What man taught a boy that the robin we'd passed—there, on the green lawn, waiting, looking around—stuck its short, sharp beak into the moist ground and plucked out gold? It is a spring morning, and I have to hurry to keep pace with my father. I am seven years old.

"I am the robin," my father says, "And you are my gold."

IV
Blowing Beauty

"Hola papá, ¿cómo estás? Right now you are going to the bathroom on the plane. I'm thinking and wondering if you were working on your book a minute ago or if you were just staring at the screen. If you were writing, what could you write about, we haven't even arrived yet. I wonder what it will be like, probably fun, how could it not be.

"I'm reading *In Cuba I was a German Shepherd*. It's really good, I recommend it to you. It's a little like *Drown*, that other book I liked so much. I was wondering about the author...I think if you're a really good writer, the reader knows you before you meet. That's why I liked *Drown*. I felt like I spent years with the main character.

"Blah blah blah, I'm just writing this so you have something to read in five minutes when I take a nap or chew some more gun. Gotta go, I'm gonna write some Spanish stuff for you to practice. I have to remember to practice Spanish on the trip. By the way, I am dying to have Mexican food, just thought I'd let you know. Well that's all for now folks. Until next plane ride, Maren."

We are flying west to join Wynton and his

band for a week, starting in San Diego. The date is June 18, a Friday, and Maren has just finished ninth grade—the day before, night before really, because she was up until about 3:30 writing the last of the papers that, cumulatively, helped her make up for some school time she had missed. Surprisingly, she does not seem tired, though I had to wake her twice for the early morning, one-hour drive to the Connecticut airport, where we caught a short flight to our connection in Newark.

Having come out by tour bus on a two-and-one-half day, nonstop drive from New York, the band (this is Wynton's quartet, with the addition of a fifth player, saxophonist Walter Blanding Jr.) has been in California since last Sunday—in Santa Barbara yesterday, Santa Cruz the day before. Wynton, who has invited Maren to come along on this trip. We were talking in Boston, where the new group was playing in Symphony Hall just four months after the *All Rise* performances, when he mentioned the idea, which Boss Murphy enthusiastically seconded.

"Let her be around some men who are doing something in their lives," Raymond had said.

Raymond, a/k/a Boss Murphy, joined Wynton's entourage almost by accident in 2000 when he got a call at his home in Washington, D.C., from his high school classmate, Wynton's longtime technical assistant and sometime roadie, Dennis Jeter (whose musical career as a trumpet player received a huge boost when he was a teenager and Wynton offered to pay his tuition at a summer music camp). A mortician by profession, as well as an active member of the Navy reserves, Raymond also has a license to operate a bus. When Wynton needed someone on short notice to drive him in the Winnebago he prefers to planes for long trips, Dennis suggested Raymond. Rock solid, a man you trust immediately based on his steady demeanor and unwavering certainty answering questions about the people and situations you encounter on the road, Boss Murphy is always on time, never complains, has a great sense of humor, and intuitively understands his place in the band. Though he knew little about jazz when he first came out on the road, he is now an expert. And Raymond *cares*; every so often, he'll sent me an email or leave me a message on my mobile phone, asking how my family is doing.

When I saw him and Wynton in Boston, just a week had passed since we'd been together briefly at a runout in Tarrytown, north of New York City. It was an early spring night, with a chill in the air, and you could feel the presence then of the Hudson River a few blocks down the historic town's Main Street from the old theater with the lights in the marquee shining brightly and the steam in the heating pipes backstage making funny noises while the band members munched on some homemade barbecue before the first set. Wynton visited with an old friend from Juilliard and then a group of school kids came in, wanting their picture taken with him, and after Wynton had obliged he let another kid hold his trumpet and told him to practice. Soon Raymond poked his head into the tiny dressing room to say, "house is ready," and Wynton asked for his horn back and very slowly walked toward the curtained stage where he lit up the full house with a fiery tune, "Free to Be," from a new CD, combining a syncopated, partly staccato, blues-based melody inflected with lots of half valve smudges and bolts of very high slurred intervals and all propelled by a swing that jumped off the stage, made you want to stand up and dance or run out into the street and shout.

That night in Tarrytown was only the second time that I'd heard the quartet, not counting a pre-Christmas gig the year before when the group played in Boston as the Ali Jackson quartet with Wynton in the unusual role as a sideman. By the following summer, reconstituted under Wynton's name and leadership, they were getting ready with engagements at small venues like the Iron Horse to record a CD of straight-ahead, mostly up-tempo, original tunes that, now, has just been released on Wynton's new label, Blue Note (where he signed after a 20-year run with Sony, nee Columbia).

Despite an historic combination of Grammys in the 1980s and the later, occasional investment of funds by Wynton himself in recording projects (he once paid $40,000 to fly his septet members back to New York, put them up in a hotel for several days, and go into the studio to re-record the score for his Garth Fagan dance collaboration *Citi Movement*), the relationship with Sony had long since soured. Sales were off, critics had for the most part responded negatively to the release of so many CDs in 1999 (nearly a dozen and a half counting the seven-CD boxed set of historic Vanguard performances), and Wynton's repeated criticism of the label's exploitation of kids through its promotion of violent and misogynist hip hop lyrics had become personal, with Wynton actually accusing at least one recording executive of living a duplicitous life, making millions for the company off recordings he would never play for his own children in his Westchester mansion.

The name of the new CD was *Magic Hour* (of which, Wynton said when he announced the title tune on stage, there are actually two—for children, the hour before they are put to bed, and for adults, the hour afterwards). *Magic Hour* is also the name of this tour that Maren and I have joined here in San Diego, where the weather is cloudy and cool as we step outside the door at the baggage claim, waiting for our luggage. From the airport, we call our hotel for a ride. A perky guy who says he's lived in the area all his life transports us in a van, talking about the city as he drives to a peninsula that juts out north of the harbor, which we can see as we look across the water. I remember that view from a trip here more than a decade before, when the septet played a gig downtown, near the marina where the sailboats for an America's Cup race were moored, on the same evening that Wynton's father Ellis was performing with former septet pianist Marcus Roberts, who is blind, at a convention for optometrists.

Almost at the tip of the peninsula, we pull over to a low-slung series of attached, wooden buildings that comprise our hotel, Humphrey's Half Moon Inn & Suites, which from early spring until late fall presents a series of concerts, most of them with pop stars.

"Hey, man," a fellow in a nice shirt and blue blazer greets me, offering his right hand, "you must be the manager."

Maren pokes me.

"Do you believe that?" Maren says,

remembering my stories about the frequency of such greetings. "Tell him you play second trumpet," she continues, but I let it go. I'm tired, Maren is hungry, and judging by the time (just after three o'clock) the band should be getting ready for soundcheck soon.

Our third-floor room looks out on a courtyard that has been set up with rows of chairs facing a stage where the musicians will play; from our vantage point, to the left of the stage you can see more water and the masts of several sailboats bobbing up and down. Maren wants to unpack before we eat, so I walk back to ground level and then along the edge of the courtyard toward the stage, veering left where I see an opening in the courtyard wall and the water beyond. With a much better view of what I now realize is a marina, I am stunned by the sheer number and size of the boats, not just sailboats but ocean-going yachts. Who owns all these boats? Where do they live? And what does a person do to earn the kind of money a toy like this can cost? I don't feel judgmental, just curious, but it's a form of curiosity that over the years I have kept to myself, or the source of it, a questioning that goes back as long as I can remember, defining who I am to myself, as opposed to the personality I present to the world.

Do other people have these secret selves, I

used to wonder, and if they did, if we all did, what prompted the secrecy? During those hikes I used to take to that hilltop in Vermont and the childhood walks to church with my father, there was always a voice within me, talking "to" me, asking question after question.

Who cleared this pasture? What happened to him?

What did the people on this street *do* behind the enormous doors of their enormous homes? Were they watching me and my father as we walked?

And what were the secret sources of my reticence to speak these questions? Was it something in my nature, some intrinsic part of whatever was just me?

The sun tries to burn off the fog as I watch the wind make little waves in the water of the marina and I decide if Maren and I are going to eat we'd better do so while we have the chance, before soundcheck. I return to our room where Maren has unpacked all her stuff and put it neatly in drawers, and we wander to the grille that also looks out on the marina and order drinks, a Coke for her and a Chardonnay for me. The waitress says if we wait a few more minutes the happy hour appetizers will be out and they are a meal in and of themselves.

Maren asks if she can order a taco, but I wait for the appetizers, not really talking with her about anything in particular, and then two men in white coats appear pushing an enormous tray of shrimp and beef.

Turns out we could both have waited a little longer and eaten with the band, which will be served dinner in a room behind the stage after a very informal soundcheck that is already underway when we return to the courtyard performance space.

"Where's Wynton?" Maren asks Carlos Henriquez, the young bass player who like Walter Blanding and pianist Eric Lewis is also a member of the Lincoln Center Jazz Orchestra. Eric is missing, too; besides Carlos and Walter, only drummer Ali Jackson is here right now.

"They're coming back from LA," Carlos says, meaning Wynton and Eric. "They were playing today at Ray Charles's funeral."

And he explains that they left for Los Angeles (where we are traveling tomorrow) early this morning, to participate in what for Wynton was something he has been doing since he was a boy, marching in funeral parades in New Orleans—a ritual commemorated subsequently in his own music in the funeral marches he has composed for such works as Six Syncopated Movements and *All*

Rise. These days, he often performs at such occasions alone, or with just his band, but this time he played with Stevie Wonder, B.B. King, Glen Campbell, and Willie Nelson in a long service held at a church with a very long name, the First African Methodist Episcopal Church.

Maren has met Walter before, in New York, when he brought his twin daughters along on a July 4th celebration several years ago in which the band took a ferry from Manhattan to a spot across the Hudson River in New Jersey not far from Ellis Island. There, against a backdrop of the twin towers of the World Trade Center, the musicians performed in a striking silhouette that took on an entirely different feeling when I remembered it after 9/11. That cataclysmic event was publicly observed by Wynton at a gig two days afterwards at the Hollywood Bowl, when he played a stirring solo national anthem before the Lincoln Center Jazz Orchestra joined the Los Angeles Philharmonic in a resonant performance of *All Rise*. The musicians then went into a Los Angeles studio to record the work, and immediately afterwards Wynton and the band left on an all-night and all-next-day bus ride to Seattle to keep a performance date that had been scheduled months before.

Like Walter, although younger, Carlos has known Wynton since he was still in high school.

His LaGuardia School for the Performing Arts band's winning participation in Jazz at Lincoln Center's annual Essentially Ellington high school band competition led him to his position today, after bassist Rodney Whitaker decided to accept a fulltime teaching position at Wayne State University in Detroit, partly in order to be at home with his large family. The shift in personnel, typical of many changes in Wynton's bands, made Rodney another member of the fraternity of former Marsalis sidemen, some of whom such as pianist Marcus Roberts and trombonist Wycliffe Gordon have gone on to solo careers and almost all of whom stay in touch with Wynton, sometimes returning on special occasions to perform again with him.

"I *live* in Detroit," Rodney said to me before leaving the band. We were enjoying cognac in the bar of a hotel in downtown Buffalo, where the Lincoln Center Jazz Orchestra had just performed on a chilly April night in the same hall where the orchestra played back when my father for a short time was its manager. Wynton had accepted my offer to drive him from the hotel to the gig in my rental car, "if I knew the way," and we'd gone right up Niagara Street, passing Johnny's Rendezvous, a speakeasy-like place where the owner used to let you in after you knocked (this was in high school) and make drinks that were so large and so strong that one lasted much of an evening. In the car I talked a little about my godfather, but Wynton seemed not to be listening, and I said nothing further to him about Buffalo while he was warming up in the same conductor's room where I used to visit Josef so many years before during those concert intermissions. The last time I'd been in this spot, I realized, was as a college student when I'd flown home for my dad's appearance as soloist with the orchestra in the Poulenc concerto, and I tried in my memory to hear the gorgeous quiet melody that comes right before that piece's climactic chords, but I could not summon that sorrowful music just then.

"I'm listening to the radio the other day," Rodney continued in Buffalo after the gig, "and this cat comes on and says whatever about business this and development that in Detroit, and then he says the city will turn around and then, '*people* will live there again.' So what does that make me and family?"

Rodney shook his head, took another sip of his drink, laughed loudly, then sighed, repeating the word again, "people!," and I told him about the time I interviewed Freddie Scott, a former wideout with the Detroit Lions, only time I was ever in Detroit other than changing planes at the airport, and did he remember Bob Lanier, I asked Rodney, played for the Pistons, All Star, biggest shoes in the NBA, size 22 I think, used to be on display in the lobby of the Basketball Hall of Fame, and Bob went to my high school I added, and check this out Rodney, *"check this out,"* yo Swigeland! I can hear Ronnie Carbo saying to me in my head, Bob Lanier didn't make our high school team the first year he tried out.

Damn.

I don't know how many children Rodney has, I mean the exact number, not because he wouldn't tell me—he loves to talk about his kids, one tour I remember he brought one of them along for a week, like Maren is here now—but it never came up. We never engaged in one of those "interviews" like I had with Freddie Scott in which I asked what books did you read in school and who was your biggest influence and how old were you when you learned to read music and then wrote something like: *It was a fall day in Detroit and wide receiver Freddie Scott felt his sore ribs and wondered if he'd be starting against the Jets this Sunday.*

Rodney and I did actually talk about books a lot, because he was always reading something on the bus and I'd be curious, what was it that he liked so much about *Tuesdays With Morrie* I might ask, and we'd be off, like when David Robinson would be on his Thomas Mann kick, or Malraux, David who collected first editions of the books he loved but read them in soft cover so the first editions would remain in excellent shape, kept them with his huge recording collection at his house in Texas, his crib but I didn't use that word; it was what had caught Wynton's attention when they first met in the late '80s, David an accountant then, coming to gigs when Wynton was in town, inviting Wynton one night after a gig to his *crib*, and Wynton thinking after he saw the collection, he told me later, "if this man who is an accountant can love these books and this music and know what he knows, he can learn how to run the sound and lights at a gig," and that is how David joined the band (and now sound technicians at some of the greatest halls in the world where the band has played ask *him* for advice). But I bet that first night when they talked Wynton never asked Rob where he went to high school, or how old his car was, or did he enjoy beer (he does). And I am sure Rob since has never said the same to Wynton, though they might *talk* about anything—women, old age, Yeats, shoes, hats, Picasso, baseball (but not Rob's favorite player, Barry Bonds, about whom no one, not even Wynton, has ever won a debate on any point with Rob).

Much as I know Maren has been looking forward to seeing Wynton, I'm almost a little relieved to realize he isn't here yet in San Diego. Though I usually pick up whatever conversation happens to be going on when I arrive and leave it wherever it happens to be when I go, it has always taken me a little time when I join the band again to readjust my bearings to the rhythms of the road. Forgetting some hard-won experience, I have more than once started a visit with a question about what horn is Wynton playing, perhaps because I know trumpet maker Dave Monette has just delivered a new one to him, or a comment on the hotel where we're staying or the food at a backstage buffet, and Wynton will look at me and cryptically reply, "You came all the way down here from Massachusetts…," or, "You came out on the road again…to ask about me about my mouthpiece?" or, "Swig, you think these mashed potatoes are interesting to talk about?"

Though I tell myself that this kind of criticism is part of the banter that signifies acceptance within the group, there were moments such as the time when Wynton introduced me at Blues Alley in Washington D.C. when I became angry. My frustration usually took the form of silent protest, like it had that night at Blues Alley, a small club in the Georgetown section of the city where Wynton had been performing since early in his career.

Ronnie Carbo had been on my case in the

van on the way over to Blues Alley from our hotel--it was when I'd been given the nickname Swig, which was actually a variant of Tre Swig, which was short for Tre Swigeland. Swig, in addition to being somewhat eponymous, was supposed to be a synonym for "piece," and Tre was an allusion to the number of women Wynton, in the front seat of the van, had announced I had slept with over the course of my repressed life. I was wearing a suit that night, with a vest, and by some happenstance was seated for the first set in the front row of the small club. When Wynton saw me there he could not resist making the connection between my clothes and my new nickname and, calling me Tre, asked me to stand so the patrons could see.

"We were just messing with you," Wynton said to me later.

"What about that time in West Virginia?" I asked.

"What about what?"

"You were finishing *In This House*, that sopranino part for Wess, and his room was next to yours so you knocked on the wall and asked him to come in--there was a door between the two rooms--and play what you had just written. Then you got tired of my questions I guess because you stopped composing and said you had to make some calls.

"'I'll see you tomorrow morning,' I said.

"'No, Swig, you got to learn to hang,' you replied. 'I'm going to call a friend in Paris.'

"And you dialed a number, ostensibly the hotel in Paris where your friend was staying, and I should have realized if that were true you were calling her at about six in the morning, Paris time, but you put on such a good performance I stayed there and listened. You called several other women, too, and it sounded like you really were talking with them, I mean the conversations were very low key and sweet.

"'That's how you call women,' you told me. 'You got to learn that, too.' And then you laughed so loudly I thought Wess was going to come back to see what was happening."

Before going to sleep that night in West Virginia we were supposed to put our bags outside our hotel room for road manager Lolis Elie to pick up for the bus, because we were leaving very early in the morning for Lexington, Virginia. Tired as I was, I remembered to leave my luggage as instructed but slept through both my alarm and the wakeup call in the morning, and the bus was fully loaded, with everyone except me on board, before Reverend Elie realized I was missing and had to knock on my door to wake me. It was the only time in my Wyntonian road life this has happened.

"Swig's been on the phone all night with a woman in Paris," Wynton announced when I appeared, bleary-eyed.

This was the same tour when we flew to San Juan for a gig that was badly promoted and Wynton got into a shouting match afterwards with the promoter who tried to blame the poor gate on the band, an incident that was forgotten later when someone with black hair and wearing a yellow dress knocked on the door of Wynton's hotel room. We'd left for Puerto Rico from North Carolina, where at a reception in the home of a university president two older women were paying a great deal of attention to Wynton and Rob.

"You should go out with them, Swig," Wynton said.

"Why is that?" I asked.

"Because they're experienced, so they will know lots of things to do."

"That's right, bruh," added Rob. "We might have to change your nickname after tonight."

At the San Diego gig an even older woman dressed in a sweater and long skirt with a floral print takes a seat near the stage just before the musicians themselves come out to enthusiastic applause, and throughout the first set this woman moves her entire body to the music, her face when I catch it from the side anticipating chord changes as she raises an eyebrow, breaks into a smile, then closes her eyes. It's chilly here, with the temperature hovering around sixty and a sea breeze blowing in from the marina. I switch locations between tunes, looking up toward the balcony where Maren has said she wants to listen from our room. Mostly, I think, she's sleepy, but she also seems intent on defining a space between the two of us, I suppose so she isn't suffocated by my enthusiasms or advice.

Where's she gone? It's between sets and I've walked up to our room to check in on her, see if she's awake, ask her if she wants to come backstage to say hi to Wynton, who got back from Los Angeles with barely enough time to change his clothes before the start of the gig. But she's not in our room. I walk over to the window and look out but certainly can't spot her in the midst of all these people sipping wine and talking below me. On the way back down, near where the stairs intersect with the entrance for concert-goers who aren't also staying at the hotel, I run into Dennis Jeter, who's along on this tour to sell some simple choices of merchandise, mostly tee shirts, and copies of the *Magic Hour* CD. Doing this represents something of a coup for Dennis because Wynton has had a longstanding policy of not promoting himself commercially at gigs; in all the years I've heard him play, not once has he ever so much as said, "And now we'd like to perform a tune from our new recording…"

Dennis—or Peter Jetey as Wynton sometimes addresses him to his great annoyance—says he thought he saw Maren a minute ago, but he's a little distracted as he discusses a sale with someone who doesn't have the exact change (everything is an even $20). Short, with a perpetual smile on his face and a voice so high it sometimes cracks, Dennis is constantly moving, as if there were no way to contain the energy in his squat body. An aspiring singer as well as accomplished trumpet player, graduate of the Manhattan School of Music and impresario of his own web-design company, Dennis two years before left New York City with his beautiful Dominican wife Betty and their two cherubic daughters for a distant suburban domain in Stroudsburg, Pennsylvania. When he's home he often works around the clock on multiple projects in a studio/office outfitted with so much high-tech gear it has the look and feel of an electronics store. He'll take a very occasional break to hit golf balls at the local driving range and he used to enjoy skiing in the winter, but with the added commute to New York and the time he spends on the road with Wynton or for his singing career he says he really has few free moments.

"Did you meet Kevin?" Dennis asks me.

"Kevin?" I reply, drawing a blank, and then I remember Raymond's phone call the day before, mentioning the number of people who would be on the tour bus and how maybe somebody might need to be in a rental car for the short San Diego-LA drive. "We've got a magician with us," Raymond told me (along with Wynton's teenage son Simeon, a friend of Simeon's, and Wynton's sort-of cousin Maurice, chef extraordinaire, formerly of New Orleans and now living in Arizona).

"Kevin's the magician?" I say to Dennis rhetorically.

"Right!" replies Dennis, who favors exclamation points in his speech.

"No, I haven't met Kevin yet, but let me find Maren first. Which way did you think she went?"

And just then, as I am beginning to fight a slight sense of anxiety, I feel a tap on my shoulder.

"Dad, there's an usher who says nobody can go backstage without a pass."

"Girl,"—how she dislikes it when I call her that—"where have you been?"

"Nowhere. Jeez."

"Well I was looking for you. Please stick around."

"Where am I going to go?"

"All right."

"Whatever."

"What did you say?"

"Nothing. I'm sorry. Dad, can we go see Wynton?"

Which we do, and will again after the second set, though we don't linger, it is late, we have been up a long time, and his suite is crowded with some people Maurice wants to introduce him to. A huge man with an even larger personality, Maurice has been showing up in Wynton's life on and off for as long as I can remember, sometimes to cook his famous gumbo, sometimes just to hang, which seems to be the case here in San Diego. We haven't been in the room together more than a few minutes before Maurice is asking me again when we're going to write that best-selling cookbook he always asks me about.

"Oh, man, it will be some kind of great cookbook!" Maurice says, squeezing my hand so hard it hurts. "Who's this beautiful woman you got with you?"

And I start to introduce him but he interrupts.

"I know this is your daughter, man. Met her that time at Wynton's."

I'm not sure which time that was. When Whitney was singing the blues after a gig? Place was crowded, Wynton had his horn out, think Wess did too, and Whitney told people her last name was Marsalis but Wynton seemed not to be bothered, nobody got hurt, nobody died, just a crazy happy moment in a lifetime of fantastic moments.

Before leaving San Diego on Saturday morning, Maren and I, still on East coast time, have an okay breakfast in the same place as we ate last night, check out, and leave our bags by the silver tour bus parked in the lot with the harbor view. It looks like no one is in a particular hurry to get going, though the band is scheduled to play tonight in the Hollywood Bowl as part of the *Playboy* Jazz Festival. According to my son, who lives in Hollywood, the hotel we're staying in is "tragically hip."

"Everything's painted white," he wrote in an e-mail, "the furniture in your room is for sale, I mean they tell you how much you can buy it for." The bar downstairs is supposed to be a scene, too, he says, especially on Saturday night.

I've been visiting LA for half my life, since my college friend Stuart, the same person who met Wynton that time at the workshop in Oakland, was living in Venice Beach and making a living as a screenwriter. I vividly remember flying into LAX at night, the lights of the vast metropolis shimmering in every direction as we prepared to land, and Stuart picked me up at the airport in his black Mazda sports car convertible with Bruce Springsteen blaring on the tape deck. Years later, after Stuart had married and moved to Israel but before my son had come out here, I arrived via tour bus with Wynton's septet, with Harold Russell at the wheel all the way from Las Vegas, where the septet had played a one-night gig after a much longer, all-night drive from Boulder, Colorado.

We stayed that time at an expensive hotel called the Westwood Marquis, a few blocks from an old theater, the Westwood Playhouse, where the septet was joined during one set by pianist Eric Reed, a preacher's son who'd played briefly with the septet after Marcus Roberts left the band. Like many band members before and after him, Eric was sent "to the woodshed," which meant home to work on his instrument. When he showed up that night in Westwood Wynton was still trying out other, new pianists, and Eric came in and played just one tune, and everyone there knew the gig was his again. It was Eric who would play the hypnotic, foot-stomping preacher's sermon near the end of *In This House,* which brought Bobby Short backstage to congratulate him after an especially exciting performance at a summer festival in Nice, France. Eventually he became restless, making remarks like renaming *Big Train*, a big-band piece of Wynton's from the mid-'90s, "Long Train."

Arriving in Los Angeles today from San Diego, Kim the driver gets off the freeway somewhere south of Anaheim and we lose some time creeping through city traffic. Kim stops for gas at a place with a paved, vacant lot adjacent to the fuel pumps, and David Robinson finds a football in the back lounge of the bus to throw around while we're waiting for the large tank to be filled. Maren, whose hand hasn't quite grown enough to grip the ball at its seams, holds it near one end but manages to make a pretty good pass to Wynton, who fires it to Rob, who tosses it back to Maren.

"Okay, girl, I'm open," Carlos hollers, running as if he were a receiver.

Maren throws a little behind him but it's still good for a completion.

"Touchdown!" someone says, but I'm only half listening, trying to reach my mother on my cell phone.

Since an emergency at Christmas, when I had to fax to her doctor a copy of her living will, my mother has been in and out of the hospital a few more times but is now, miraculously, living at home—frail and not yet able to walk—with my sister in a small coastal town north of Portland, Maine. At Easter I visited with Maren and my wife and we all went out to dinner at a seafood place; just before this trip I went up again with my older daughter Anna, home for the summer from circus school in Montreal , and we pushed my mother in her wheelchair on a long walk down to the tidal river a half mile or so from my sister's. It was a sunny afternoon, a little chilly for June, and with the talk in the news about the anniversary of D-Day I found myself asking my mother again about the time she met my uncle at the train station in New York after he was released from Walter Reed Hospital.

"We went out for dinner then," she said, a fact she had not before shared with me. "And then we went dancing at the New Yorker. There were lots of places in those days, where you could dance."

"But I thought he was still so weak," I said, meaning my uncle, a p.o.w. in World War II.

"He was," my mother replied, and then stopped speaking for a few minutes, lost in her recollection. We had reached a spot on the path by the river that overlooked some falls, and we watched the water running over the rocks. On the return we stopped for ice cream cones at the corner store on the town's Main Street.

"We're supposed to be there already but I think we may be lost," I'm saying to my mother now, as I watch Maren run across the pavement for a pass from Rob.

"Yeah, she's fine, we're both still a little tired but we got lots of sleep. Christian's meeting us when we get to the hotel. He's coming to the concert tonight, then tomorrow's an off day, no travel either, we don't leave for Albuquerque until two a.m. Monday. Yeah, that'll be a long ride, twelve hours I think and we're only there overnight and then it's on to Santa Fe. I love you, too. Let me put Maren on."

Back on the bus it soon becomes clear that we are not only lost but we're going to be late. Oblivious to "where" we are—*fact is: we are on a bus*—Wynton has been arguing with Eric Lewis about the availability of images on the internet of Iraqi hostages and, more specifically, of the beheading of an American hostage. Only half tuned into the debate, which if I'm following it correctly focuses in part on Eric's insistence that the power of such an image to repulse resides only within the viewer, I have been keeping an eye out for familiar landmarks while trying also to keep a little distance from my daughter, who is more than holding her own as the only female among 14 passengers and Kim the driver (earlier plans to lighten the load by adding that rental car were dropped, no reason given; no questions, as I learned long ago on the road, asked). When I am sure the direction we're going is west, not east, I break another rule of the road and, indirectly, comment on someone else's job by mentioning to Boss Murphy that I think we're heading toward Santa Monica and the Pacific Ocean, not Beverly Hills and Hollywood.

"Let me check with Kim, " Raymond says, and in a few minutes we've reversed our course. I call my son to confirm our route, but not our arrival time, having quickly sensed I've already strayed as far as I should: we'll get there when we get there.

By now Wynton and Eric have transposed their conversation to music, and Wynton is recalling when he started to *hear* saxophonist Sonny Rollins. The key word, Wynton is saying, is *intent*, as in what was Sonny's intent?

"And when you've peeped something like that out," Wynton says, citing his discovery of Sonny's intent in the soundtrack he composed for the Michael Caine film *Alfie*, "when that happened for me with Sonny, I couldn't wait to get back to my hotel room after a gig to listen. It was the same when I first heard *Giant Steps* and started to peep out Trane. I wanted to rush home from school and listen to it again. And it's so rare now, to have three or four musicians of the caliber of that band in the same room together at the same time."

The discussion morphs to Wynton's own work, including *All Rise*, which Eric has been learning for a repeat performance next month with the Boston Symphony Orchestra, this time at Tanglewood (in what, so far as I can tell, will be the first-ever presentation there of a single work written by a living composer and comprising an entire program). There is a direct relationship, Wynton is saying, between the chord progressions of his much earlier *In This House, On This Morning* and *All Rise*, one of many aspects of his work, he laments in a later conversation, "that no one has bothered to explain. No one listens to *In This House*," he continues. "But it will come around."

Eric, whose place in the Boston performances of *All Rise* was taken by 17-year-old Juilliard student Aaron Diehl, has apparently put aside whatever objections he had to the work's text, which Wynton also wrote. His focus seems to have shifted to the meaning of the music.

"I really put something in that first movement," Wynton says in a rare boast, but his explication of the score is cut short because we have finally arrived at the Mondrian Hotel in West Hollywood, after a four-hour drive that should only have taken two. No one complains, in fact no one else seems to have noticed. *Fact is: we are here.*

Well, almost. Perhaps because of the high

cost of real estate at this end of Sunset Boulevard, the Mondrian has been constructed with a minimum of space between the front exterior of the building and the curb. So, to stop the bus where bellhops can unload the luggage while other guests are pulling in and out of the valet parking area is difficult. Kim decides to deal with this after we all get off, because Raymond has already returned from the lobby with room keys for everyone; he even has mine and Maren's, with the understanding that when we check out we'll explain to the front desk that the charges go on my card, not the band's.

"Nice!" exclaims Maren, when we get to our room. "Very cool."

The walls and all the furniture are indeed white, with white curtains framing two large windows that look out in the direction of the city's vast, distant downtown. Maren immediately begins to unpack and she's still carefully laying out her various creams and sprays in the bathroom when there's a knock on the door signaling the arrival of her brother.

Ten years older than Maren, Christian left home when she was still in elementary school—he came out here two days after his college graduation. Until recently a production assistant at *South Park*, Christian's been working the past few months at a small talent agency nearby, while continuing to write a screenplay at night and during whatever weekend time he isn't either biking or working at a bike shop by the water. He was at the bike shop today, but took off early to meet us when we called to say we were getting close.

"You guys eaten yet?" Christian asks.

Even if we had, I know Maren's response would have been the same enthusiastic, "Where shall we go?"

Christian says there's a place, Saddle Ranch, practically across the street.

"We can sit outside," he adds—which is what we do, at a table perched on a sidewalk in a space so close to the street you feel you could reach out and touch a passing car.

"I don't know what the deal will be tonight," I say. "The last time I was there it was so crowded backstage no one really got any food." I don't need to repeat another road rule: *Eat when you can.* We each order an early dinner.

"Something to drink?" I ask my son, expecting him to ask for beer.

"Water's fine," he says.

"California," I think, remembering but not mentioning my surprise when I arrived at Stuart's that time in Venice Beach and he had installed in his apartment an electronic device he called an air ionizer.

Two hours later we're waiting in the lobby of the Mondrian for Boss Murphy to give the signal that the vans to take everyone to the Hollywood Bowl are ready. One by one the band members saunter down, and we have more company, too.

"Miller!" I shout, addressing Wynton's Tennessee friend, John Miller, a sometime filmmaker, writer, and all around go-to guy who just shows up wherever—often New York, and usually having just had a drink, or two, or on his way to get one. In New York a few years ago, on a winter's night, I had stopped at Wynton's after a rehearsal and Miller was visiting, and there was nothing to drink. It was late, too.

"I know a place that will be open," Miller said, so I followed him up Amsterdam Avenue, past a closed liquor store, and we continued in the bitter cold, the wind blowing, for several more blocks beyond where Amsterdam crisscrosses with Broadway, until finally we were in luck.

"Let's get some Sherry," Miller intoned. "Skain's been liking Sherry."

So I bought a bottle of something, can't recall what but it was expensive, and we brought it back with us, and then I was afraid I was going to miss my train at that point—I was staying at my brother's, just outside the city—so I left. When I came by the next night the bottle was empty.

In the Mondrian this night Miller is talking with Wynton's dapper doctor friend from New Orleans, Ken Mast, whom everyone addresses simply as K., and who has just self-published his first book, a mystery, and who is also Miller's occasional film collaborator, in fact they've recently completed a project with another friend of Wynton's named Todd Williams, not the Todd Williams who used to play tenor sax in the septet but someone who lives out here and works in the movie industry.

"Have you seen our movie?" K. asks me.

"Which movie is that?" I reply.

"The N-word documentary," John interjects. "Damn, Veeglan, you got to see this one, this is a bad-ass film." And then he lowers his voice a little, as if to share a confidence, and puts a hand on one of my shoulders. "You know the N-word, Veeglan? You know what that is?" And he sort of howls and smiles and slaps me on the back. "Damn, you got to see this one!"

Except for Wynton the band is assembled now in the lobby and Raymond tells them to take the first van and we'll see them there.

"What's Wynton's room number?" I ask and then head upstairs in the elevator with Christian and Maren. K. Mast comes along, too, but Miller remains in the lobby. He's started a conversation with a couple of young women who wonder who these musicians are and is this the gig they have tickets for they ask though it is pretty clear they don't have tickets to anything nor the slightest inclination to purchase them.

"Great One," K. humorously greets Wynton, who is still ironing his shirt while Simeon and his younger brother, Wynton's third son Jasper, who lives out here with his mother, finish room-service burgers in the adjoining room while watching a baseball game on television without the sound. In less than half an hour Wynton is supposed to be performing before more than 20,000 people at the Hollywood Bowl, but from his demeanor you would think he is getting reading to attend a meeting of the PTA at Jasper's school.

"Hey, little Swig," Wynton addresses Christian. "What's happening?"

Then the phone rings.

"Yass, yass, thank you, we're on our way right now," Wynton fibs to Boss Murphy. It's another five minutes before we are out the door and soon stuck in stop-and-go traffic on Hollywood Boulevard.

In the front seat, with Jasper sitting on his lap, Wynton takes his mouthpiece out and starts playing a few drills on it to warm up.

"Sorry, boss," he says to the driver. "How long a drive we got?"

"Can't tell, this traffic."

"Anyone know what time we go on?" Wynton asks. Not waiting for an answer, he continues playing a tune on his mouthpiece while the van creeps uphill toward the venue. Jasper tickles one of his father's armpits and Wynton feigns a blank expression, as if he were a wax figure, and then breaks into laughter. When we finally turn at the entrance we bypass hundreds of cars double and triple parked and pull up to a gate backstage, where we follow Boss Murphy to a lady at a table who is dispensing passes. With Jasper in tow, Wynton has disappeared through a stage door, and before we have found our way into the amphitheater we can hear master of ceremonies Bill Cosby introducing him as the floor of a revolving stage makes a semi-circle, so rather than walking out the band simply appears suddenly, having been seated on the hidden side of the stage as Cosby spoke and then emerging while they begin playing.

The mixed, boisterous crowd, which has been here for several hours eating and drinking and listening to other acts, erupts in a prolonged ovation. Folks in the lower portion of the bowl are seated at tables that are roped off from the upper seats and watched over by zealous ushers.

"Follow me," K. says, and when an usher asks to see our tickets he tells her he's a doctor and we continue to the front section, a little to one side, where an older guy eyes us suspiciously as we find an empty table.

I don't like it down here, so close to the giant speakers on either side of the recently renovated stage, the speakers necessary I gather because the amphitheater space is so large. The amplification seems designed more for a rock band, so there is a tinny, hollow sound to acoustic instruments; even the piano sounds canned.

"Let's move," I say to my kids, and we are soon standing in the cross aisle that separates the upper and lower sections of the bowl, which is literally carved out of a hill and, were we to climb to its top, would I imagine present a vast view of the city, like it looked that time I flew into LAX at night. An usher asks us to move, and we walk now to the side, where the smell of marijuana mixes with the fragrances of many perfumes and the aroma of food.

On the clock, with a directive not to go over because another act is waiting to follow, the band plays a short set, and Wynton keeps his stage chatter brief. He's played here many times over the years and it's always a challenge to know what will work. When he played *Big Train* at the 2000 festival many in the audience tuned out; it was the wrong piece for this venue.

"We'd like to conclude with two songs for the memory of two musicians," he says now, and he announces their names—Ray Charles and the jazz drummer Elvin Jones, with whose band Wynton had once toured Japan (and with whom he recorded some of the music on his 1991 three-CD blues cycle, *Soul Gestures in Southern Blue*). The two tunes are a stirring version of "Rugged Cross" and a New Orleans-style arrangement of "Down by the Riverside," during which many people in the crowd wave handkerchiefs in the air, as if they were second-lining in the Crescent City.

An old man with his handkerchief leads several other men and women in a spontaneous parade toward the front of the bowl, and some of the women raise parasols up and down as they move to the rhythm of the music. The cheering that comes at the end sounds more like what you would hear at a sporting event, loud yells and cries for more.

Afterwards, Wynton deals with the usual backstage LA throng, which also includes Jasper's mom, to whose home Wynton is going later. I am about to tell him what a sad display the set was when I sense he is already someplace else, the brief braggadocio an uncharacteristic cover for the complex of emotions he must be dealing with at this moment, with the mother of one of his children nearby, a gaggle of wannabees competing for his patient attention, the usual myriad of problems elsewhere to deal with (focused this time on raising the remaining capital for the new hall in New York; completing the program plans for the first season), and the long part of this tour still ahead, with gigs in St. Louis, Cleveland, and Montreal after Colorado, which is as far as Maren and I are going. None of this is ever mentioned in conversation, nor the painful cyst on his upper lip (that will eventually force him to cancel the Montreal gig, a distressing first in his career).

Another backstage visitor, seated in his wheelchair and greeting friends as if he, too, had been performing, is D.J. Riley. D.J. has just moved back to Los Angeles after spending the past year or so in New Jersey, near his parents, following the death of his sister from Morquios syndrome, the same disease that has incapacitated D.J.'s body (another sibling, a brother, is healthy). His sister's last wish, D.J. said, was to attend a Jazz at Lincoln Center concert and meet Wynton, which she was able to do shortly before she died after D.J. got in touch with Billy Banks, Wynton's first road manager, who in the old days did everything from making hotel reservations to driving the band's van.

"That meant so much to her," D.J. told me, when I had visited him two years ago in his home here in LA before he left for New Jersey. Driving over from my son's on a sunny afternoon to a neighborhood near but not in the city's South Central section, I had turned onto a tidy street of nearly identical bungalow-design houses, each with its own driveway and unattached garage. Separated from the street by a weedless lawn, D.J.'s one-story, brick house looked unoccupied from the front, with the windows curtained and the door locked, but around back a nurse on her way to do errands greeted me cheerfully and told me to let myself in, I'd find D.J. in his room in the rear.

With only his head visible above a shroud of sheets and blankets, he was seated near the end of his bed in a wheelchair that had been retrofitted with various devices to help him answer and talk on his phone and to manipulate his nearby television and computer with voice-recognition commands and signals that he made by blowing into various tubes. The walls of the bright, sunlit room were lined with shelves piled high with medical supplies. Throughout our hour-long conversation, there was a constant stream of calls from people in Los Angeles and elsewhere in the country. And at one point D.J. made a call himself to a radio station where he said he was going to be hosting some kind of talk show, if I got the story right. With clarity and passion, he moved quickly from one topic to the next, interweaving his observations with frequent quotes and illustrating his points with regular references to musicians and their music, including the young musicians with whom Wynton was always working:

"Art is something that is not only beautiful in itself but is something that connects with the needs and desires and hopes of the people that need it. It molds itself to provide a tool, a mechanism for us to uplift ourselves and strengthen ourselves and the people we care about.

"I'm optimistic. Still. After forty-two years.

"Do you concentrate on what isn't in your life and blame your shortcomings and your troubles on what isn't?

"Or do you find a way to take the pieces of life that God has given you and maximize them to some kind of joy, maximize them to show how more can be made out of little--if one's desires and motivations are to add?"

Sunday morning, early, quiet streets, cloudy sky. Maren's still asleep back in our room on the fold-out couch, that breakfast place Frank Stewart and I went to one time, Duke's, is too far to walk, and I will have to settle again for Starbucks, with a stop at my favorite Sunset Boulevard bookstore for newspapers. It's pleasantly cool at this hour, but maybe not comfortable I decide to sit outside. I must remember to get something to take back for Maren and to call Christian, see if he's up yet, ask him where can we all have brunch?

Last night, coming back to the Mondrian, most of us were packed into one van, with Jasper and his dad again sitting in the front seat. The two women Miller had met earlier, who had managed to hustle a ride to the venue in one of the vans, had disappeared after they had been given tickets that, someone said, "they probably scalped." This certainly hadn't fazed Miller, who was in rare form in the back of the van, talking so loudly that Wynton finally asked him to quiet down, which he did not do.

"John, I'm gonna *dis* you if you won't stop," piped up Jasper.

Then they went back and forth, Jasper continuing to repeat his "dis" threat, all the way to the Mondrian, where Miller headed straight for the outdoor pool and terrace, which had been turned into a giant bar. The bouncer wouldn't let Maren in.

"That's okay, Dad, I'm tired," Maren said. "I just want to watch a little TV and go to sleep."

So, my son and I joined Miller for a drink, and he proceeded to introduce us both to some women he didn't know. We were standing near a railing at a corner of the terrace, the three of us, and Miller turned to the strangers next to us, offered to buy them a drink, and then said, "Please say hello to my friends here," and then disappeared. We left, too, a little while after that.

"What time is that Dodgers-Yankees game?" I'm asking my son now, on Sunday, late morning, at this Mexican place we've come to for brunch.

"It's a sellout," Christian replies, but I'm undaunted. The Yankees are Maren's team, and I have a vivid memory of taking Christian to Chavez Ravine, the Dodgers' ballpark, when he was an infant and we were visiting Stuart.

"I think it's a late start," I say, "for television back east." I can't understand why I didn't check in the newspaper earlier, but in Christian's car I call the box office.

"Five o'clock!" I announce. "Do you want to go? Someone will be selling tickets."

With very little further discussion we decide to give it a shot. It's a fairly short drive from where Christian lives, and he says he knows how to avoid the freeway. We leave his apartment for the ballpark at three and can see its light towers ahead in less than half an hour. What if we can't get in? Or what if the only tickets being scalped are hundreds of dollars a piece?

Somehow certain this baseball game idea is going to work, I scan the neighborhood for signs of scalpers, and then I remember that in Los Angeles everyone drives everywhere and that here in Chavez Ravine you park your car in a lot located near an entrance on the same level as your seats. There are no scalpers until we begin inching forward in the traffic lanes that lead toward the lots, which surround the park and are fenced in. All scalping transactions, I finally grasp, must be conducted from your moving car, before you reach the gate.

"Watch your wallet, Carl," Christian says. It's what he's always called me—my first name.

I'm sitting in the seat next to him and I can see several men holding tickets in the air. As soon as I put the window down they start elbowing one another for the chance to make a sale. Afraid we may miss out, I buy the first trio of tickets that someone offers, at a relatively small markup, and not until we've moved forward and I've looked at them do I realize they are not together. I jump out of the car and run back to the scalper who sold them to me.

"Nothing I can do about it, man" he says. "Just hold them like this"—and he shows me how to hide the seat section identification on the odd ticket—"and he'll let you in the same entrance." Then he turns away to make another transaction and I have to sprint to catch up with Christian's car.

The little scam about the entrance works, despite the fact that the ticket whose section identification I am disguising is for an entirely different level, and we walk around the beautiful park along the right field foul line to the place where two of our seats are located and where, 25 years earlier, Christian had attended his first baseball game perched on my chest in a Snugly. For the first inning, no one is sitting in the adjacent row, and I'm able to enjoy the game with Christian and Maren while remaining wary that I may have to move. In the top half of the second a group of people begin to file into the empty row, and as I stand up I explain my predicament.

"That's cool," the young man next to us says. "My buddy's not here yet. Me and my girl will move over one."

"Let me buy you a beer," I say.

"You don't have to do that. But thanks."

The rest of the game passes in a kaleidoscopic blur. Maren's favorite player, Derek Jeter, hits a home run, but the Dodgers win. On the way out she and I apply for Dodgers Visa cards in order to receive free Dodgers tee shirts.

"What should I put down for assets?" she asks me as she fills out the required application.

"Make it up," Christian says.

I'm feeling wistful about our imminent departure, though it's several hours away. I remember the first time I visited after Christian moved out here, when he was renting a one-bedroom apartment he could not really afford. We drove to Palm Springs, where I had a magazine assignment, and he got sick, couldn't swallow food his throat was so sore. We drove back without conversation and I was tempted to change my departure flight because of his health.

"I'll be okay," he insisted, in a whispered tone that I interpreted as, "I'm on my own now, really, you can head home."

And so I did, leaving very early the next morning, still dark when I started for the airport and, following his directions, drove much of the way on city streets instead of the freeway, parts of sleeping Los Angeles a ghost town that mingled with my mood, the ghosts of my first-born's receding childhood chasing one another in my memory, summer nights when we played baseball after dinner in the field behind the barn and I could still remember the first time he hit one on the fly into the neighbor's lawn, and the winter when he wanted to learn to skate and a friend at the prep school in the next town said he could skate on Saturday mornings with the faculty kids, said we could both come actually if I'd help out, so I became a hockey coach and he got so hooked on hockey we started going to the games at the school, we'd drive down late on a weekday afternoon, they usually began at four, and between periods we'd run across the street to the local market that sold coffee and hot chocolate and usually still had some doughnuts left, and when I got the golf bug he did, too, joining me if I promised to rent a cart, which he would drive; sometimes we'd take a picnic along with us and park the cart in the rough near the woods by the covered bridge over the brook between the seventh green and eighth tee; he'd go to concerts with me, too—when I was working on a book set in Boston he came along sometimes, once I remember on the return home complaining about the cigarettes I still smoked then and soon after that, on a solo trip, I stopped at a Burger King on the Massachusetts Turnpike for a very lousy late-night snack and when I reached into my pocket afterwards there was just one cigarette in the pack, crumpled, and I looked at it, fingered it, smelled it...and threw it away with the remains of my meal, and have never smoked another one since.

    Leaving Chavez Ravine, traffic so bad we

don't move in the parking lot for more than half an hour, Maren says, "I'm hungry," and Christian says, "I know a good place for Mexican takeout," and so we drive there in the June dusk, it's nearly nine o'clock by the time we find it, and we each order burritos, which we bring back to Christian's apartment, stopping en-route for a bottle of wine and I treat my son (and myself) to something good, which we open to have with the burritos.

Maren takes one bite of hers and looks at me as if to say, "Is yours okay?"

The chicken is overly charred, the sour cream and salsa don't seem fresh, the taco itself is a little stale.

I take a sip of the wine and ask Maren if she'd like to try a little.

"Sure!"

Then we return, grim-faced, to our burritos.

Finally Christian speaks up.

"I don't think these are happening," he admits.

Maybe we can get a snack at the hotel. Or, for Maren and me, there will be food on the bus, which is now not departing for New Mexico until three a.m. because everyone except Wynton is playing a gig that Ali Jackson arranged at a local club. Since he has to be at work the next morning, Christian says he won't be able to stay up that late with us, so after watching part of a lousy DVD from his roommate's vast collection, we start back for the Mondrian.

With our budget for the trip in mind, I checked out earlier and left our bags with the concierge. It's close to midnight now and the Mondrian's dining room is closed. Bribing him with a small tip, I persuade the bartender at the adjacent terrace to let us sit at a table in the empty, darkened dining room.

There isn't a lot to say. We're tired, and Maren and I have several more hours to stay awake. Christian tells me a little more about his latest screenplay, a thriller for a small production company where he started as an unpaid script reader, and we laugh about the treatment for a television series we wrote together the year before, which in the labyrinth of Hollywood politics basically never made it past my agent.

"We really needed a pilot," Christian says, and I nod. The idea for the show was a kind of golf *Cheers*, set at a fictitious resort on an island in the Caribbean. The main character was a man named Benny Motion, a teaching pro at the resort's golf course, divorced with two kids who live with his former wife back in Florida, where Benny had failed to earn a living as a competitor in mini-tour events. His sidekick was a guy named Peter

Madison, which was the name I gave to my surrogate character in many of the unpublished short stories I wrote on those early mornings at the dining room table when we lived on the dairy farm when my wife was pregnant with Christian.

"I should really be going," Christian says.

"I know," I reply, staring at him, six feet tall, a very lean 190 pounds, his hair still blond, his eyes my father's blue.

We walk to his car, which the valet said as a favor he could park free by the curb, since it was quiet this Sunday night.

"You take care," I say, realizing with a sudden start that we probably won't see him again until Christmas; he's already told us he won't get a vacation this summer, having started his new job at the agency so recently.

"'Bye, Christian," Maren says, giving her brother a last hug. And he's gone.

"If you can't play the blues,'" Wynton said the other night, quoting Lester Young, "'you can't play shit.'"

Or leave Los Angeles long after midnight, the streets of the city seeming to pass by us instead of our moving through them, traffic lights changing, an occasional car or truck ahead, not a person out walking so far as I notice. Inside the bus's crowded front lounge, the talk begins with baseball, with Rob expounding on Ken Griffey Jr., and then we shift briefly to golf, why didn't Tiger win the U.S. Open that just concluded, Wynton asks, not really caring, I think, from the sound of his voice but he knows I follow the sport. In between bursts of conversation I listen to the soothing sound of the wheels on the pavement, a kind of steady hum against the drone of the gears when they are shifting, peaceful somehow even though they are propelled by a machine; the sound and the sense of a lighted, closed place, a secure environment, creates and then reinforces the feeling that we are not simply moving on but like the music putting behind us whatever we just did, whatever we just experienced, good or bad, happy or sad, it's gone, over, and we are physically traveling toward tomorrow.

Carlos, who along with Ali thought about flying to Albuquerque because the bus is so full, is bummed about the gig at the Hollywood Bowl. Constantly questioning himself and the band like this, Carlos couldn't really hear on stage he says, by which he means hear the other members of the band, but he also wonders what the audience heard. He couldn't pick up its vibe, all those people and the big stage.

"It is what it is," Wynton says, too tired for

a prolonged conversation just now, and still it seems affected by whatever went on after the gig, though he won't say anything about it; if there is a response, it will come in the music at the next gig, or in what he is writing just now (a long delayed piece to be premiered this winter during Jazz at Lincoln Center's first season it its new hall). Dennis Jeter and Ali have already made their way to the triple-tiered bunks in the middle section of the bus, and Walter looks ready to follow them.

"How're you doing?" I ask Maren, who was drooping during the last hour at the hotel but has now revived.

"I'm fine, Dad. Go to sleep."

So I do, stretching out on one side of the rear lounge, my favored napping place ever since I got claustrophobic on a septet tour when, sleeping in a floor-level bunk on a night-time ride through the Rockies, I awoke to use the john and realized when I went forward to say hello to Harold Russell that we were in the midst of a snowstorm. All I could think about after that was being in that bottom bunk with the bus rolling over. Of course that never happened, not with the world's greatest bus driver at the wheel…but once the idea lodged itself in my mind I couldn't get rid of it, like a tune you start humming to yourself and can't stop.

*

Well into the morning, the sensation of slowing down triggers something in my unconscious. Blinking, I peer out through one of the blinds to a startling brightness, the air clear, some kind of conifer near the place we've parked, and from other trips and my own inner gyroscope I conclude we must be somewhere in the vicinity of Flagstaff, Arizona. Kim confirms this after I pass through the quiet darkness of the bunks, with no one including Maren stirring, to the front of the bus, where Rob has been watching a movie.

Outside at this truck stop the air is also quite cool and I wish I were wearing a sweater, but it feels good to be walking a few steps, moving my arms, taking deep breaths. I wonder what Christian is doing. Must be on his way to work. I'm about to call him but I then think no, let him be. I'm thirsty and a little hungry and could kill for some coffee though I don't imagine the stuff they sell here will be anything to rave about.

How true.

In less than two hours we are crossing the Arizona desert, and just about noon we enter New Mexico, where there's another truck stop at which Kim has to pay a special tax. Everyone's awake now, an old DeNiro flick is playing, even Wynton is watching it while he gives Simeon, sitting next to him, a backrub.

"Longest drive I ever remember was twenty-two hours," Dennis Jeter says. "Winnipeg, Canada to Interlaken, Michigan. We were in a Winnebago, I took turns driving and Wynton had us listening to a book on tape, it was either the *Odyssey* or the *Iliad*."

By mid-afternoon we're approaching downtown Albuquerque, and Rob starts talking about the promoter for tonight's gig here and tomorrow night's in Santa Fe.

"Bumble Bee Bob," Rob says, his lips puckering on the alliterated B's. And then he repeats the first word, annunciating slowly: "Bum-ble-bee!"

The bus pulls to the curb, the door swings open, and waiting to greet us is the very person whose name Rob has been having fun saying, a bundle of energy in his late 60s with a yellow cap on his head, the cap decorated with the oversize likeness of a bee.

"Bumble Bee!" Wynton says with a smile, as if this word were part of a chorus. And right at that moment I realize I know this man, just not his nickname. He was a cattle rancher when I met him more than 20 years ago, interviewed him in Santa Fe for a magazine article, visited his enormous ranch with its house up on a hill outside town with views in every direction of the mountains, came home and told my wife if we ever decided to move

I had found the place. Bob Weil is his real name, and he's a concert promoter now—and a restaurateur, I'll learn tomorrow when the food after soundcheck is catered from the "beestro," Bumble Bee's Baja Grill, that he and his inspirational second wife B.J. began two years ago.

"Howdy," he says to the new musicians he hasn't met before, while Wynton and Rob—and me—are greeted with bear hugs.

"Dad," Maren interrupts, "I seriously need a shower." And so we head up to our room, with its view of a downtown sculpture park that I explore after the desk clerk I call tells me no, this Hyatt doesn't have wireless internet yet but some people say you can pick up the city's free connection in the park.

No such luck, and once again I settle for Starbucks, where I can't decide whether or not to have an extremely late and not very nutritious breakfast or be patient and wait for an early, possibly more balanced supper. And then I realize we've lost an hour, we're on central time now, and will there even be time before the gig for food?

The recently renovated KiMo Theatre, a short walk from our hotel, is a curious blend of art deco and Native American iconography. Backstage, on a stairway landing, a kind of open closet serves as a shrine to someone named Bobby who, an inscription reads, "was killed in this building in 1951." No explanation, no other details. The band is playing two sets tonight, with our magician Kevin Lee opening the second with several sight gags. The house is packed for both sets and clamors for an encore at the end of the second. Wynton obliges with an extended solo blues, some of it played so quietly it's as if Wynton were whispering through his horn.

"I really got to something there," he says later, in response to a compliment, but this is as far as he ever goes in trumpet talk. Quickest way to end a musical conversation with him is to say something like, "That was cool, the way you turned that trill on the low C and B into a rhythmic figure for the following phrase."

"What trill? What phrase?"

To my disappointment, Maren misses the blues. She's been hanging out with Simeon and his friend, and all three of them are ravenously hungry as the gig concludes.

"I'll walk with them back to the hotel and we'll get some food there," I say to Boss Murphy.

"Okay," he responds in a clipped, almost staccato voice, as if he had for a second thought this was one of his Navy reserve weekends. He's helping Rob deal with the folders of music and the wiring onstage while keeping an eye out for

Wynton, who is supposed to make an appearance in the lobby to meet some of the benefactors of an area jazz foundation that Bumble Bee helped found and to which he has donated generously.

When the four of us get back to the hotel the dining room is closed, but the bartender says the teenagers can order off the appetizer menu, so we take seats at a table large enough to accommodate the four of us and saxophonist Walter Blanding, who was asking at the theater where he could eat. Conversation until Walter's arrival consists of chit-chat about sports and school; I remember from Christmas the year before, when Simeon was along when his father was a sideman at the Ali Jackson gig in Boston, that Simeon had more or less stopped doing his school work for a while, and I ask him now is he back to his books?

Smiling, he shrugs, passes as well on a question about the clarinet, and reports that his older brother Wynton Jr. is still playing soccer. There's a lot of pent-up energy in Simeon, always has been, and I ask him about his chess. Until recently he was beating his father regularly, but then Wynton started playing a lot, at home as well as on the road, and the matches have become closer.

"I let him win sometimes," Simeon says, and laughs. His eyes dart around the room. "Think that hamburger will be here soon?"

Before I can answer the waitress appears with the food, almost simultaneously with the arrival of Walter, who orders a plate of baby-back ribs. He sits at the opposite end of the table from me, with our young guests between, so it's a little difficult to make out every word as we catch up on bits of family news. The son of musicians, born in Cleveland but raised mostly on Staten Island, where his parents moved when he was ten, Walter's in his early 30s. He lived in Israel for several years with his first wife, the mother of his twin daughters, and he's married now to a woman from Italy. In addition to playing in two of Wynton's bands he's earning a degree at the New School in Manhattan, where he lives. It's a complicated life, but you always get a sense when you're talking with Walter that he sees the clear line, stays focused on what follows, whether it's to meet his daughters after school or visit his mother, who has remarried since the death of his father and to whom Walter bears such a striking resemblance that they could pass for brother and sister. Walter speaks in a clear, cadenced voice, filled with both empathy and joy, which are the qualities beyond the extraordinary technical skill that immediately strike you when he's playing the saxophone.

Pianist Eric Lewis must have had Walter in mind when he gave me his definition of jazz. "Jazz music," says Eric, "is the sound of someone's dance sensibility."

This is the same Eric who earlier this past spring, in a gig at the Troy Savings Bank Hall in Troy, New York, brought the audience to its feet in a standing ovation *during* a tune—it was after a long improvisation in which he more or less surveyed the entire history of jazz piano, segueing from stride to ragtime to swing to blues, all in one improvisation lasting perhaps 20 minutes, with gradations of volume and velocity, complicated chord changes with stretched fingerings that had to have challenged even his enormous hands, and all within a logic of rhythm and form that gave the improvisation not simply an aesthetic coherence but an artistic inevitability.

And so in Santa Fe, the night after Albuquerque, *I'll Remember April* is the tune in the first set when Eric takes off again, the whole band does, Walter and Carlos and Ali and Wynton, nothing like what they just played in San Diego or Los Angeles and yet the very same core, nothing's changed in that, the heart of Saturday's "Rugged Cross" is now the base of "Blues in Bogey," and how I wish Maren were sitting with me behind one side of the opened curtain, onstage, where I can see and hear the band but the audience cannot see me, my preferred place to sit, the spot I've always claimed going all the way back to that gig in Nebraska when Wynton invited that old woman to sit with the band on stage and when I commented on it afterwards invited me to do so, too, but I concluded that I liked it better in the secluded, darkened intimacy of the stage-wing, where once at a gig in Hartford, Connecticut, Billy Banks who was road managing a runout and his wife Laurie stood, not sat, in the same place between tunes and as soon as the music began again they danced, just the two of them, there on the hidden side of the stage, and another time I remember was in South Carolina, Greenville was the name of the town, where we'd arrived after a long day's drive from Durham, where Wynton had played a long blues with a young boy at a school assembly, and then in Greenville backstage during soundcheck I'd started a conversation with a member of the theater's staff, think she may have gone to the university whose theater it was, Furman its name, anyway she had never before heard jazz and so I was telling her about that tour, remarking on the interplay between Wynton and Wycliffe Gordon, the extreme degree of their coordination and the intensity of hearing that it required, and not just hearing of course but also of responding, I meant how they heard and then responded to one another, funny word, respond, made it seem a little academic, but

Tami I believe her name was responded to what I said and so we continued the conversation afterwards, my father was stationed near here when he was in training camp during the Second World War I said, right up the road more or less and she said where and I said Spartanburg and she said yes it's not that far and I asked did she know a town north of Spartanburg, it was actually just over the state line in North Carolina, town was called Tryon, and Tami said she'd heard of it but never been there and why did I ask, and I said, "That's the town where my father moved before he died."

Wynton, playing a solo at the end of a tune by Coleman Hawkins during the second set in Santa Fe, sounds a high wail and then segues to a New Orleans march, moves momentarily into a melody before unfurling a blazing sequence of arpeggios, finally finishes with a kind of whistle, and all the while, sitting next to me now, having missed the entire first set because she volunteered to return to the hotel half a block away…to fold Wynton's laundry…Maren taps her feet while she listens, and then in *My Ideal* Maren moves her head and her shoulders.

"Let's walk the other way," I say after the gig, outside the theater, and I mean let's walk a few blocks in the other direction from the hotel to the square, where some of the oldest buildings in North America cast a mystical spell on this clear night: so many stars visible here in these hills! More interested in the closed shops we pass than the historic church at the center of the square, Maren runs ahead on the return, reminding me again very briefly but very sharply that she's fifteen, not fifty. Again on the next day's ride to Denver I realize this when, driving by Colorado Springs with towering, snow-capped Pike's Peak looming over the high, western horizon, I try to catch her attention.

"Look, Maren, the Rockies!"

"Yes, Dad?" she says, looking up from the CD she's selecting for her Walkman.

At Loews Denver Hotel, located in the southern end of the city, several miles from downtown, she comes to life when she notices a strip mall within what she perceives as walking distance. With a promise that she'll stay in touch with me on her cell phone, she negotiates permission to visit the stores across the street.

"Remember we have to eat here at the hotel before the gig," I tell her, because Boss Murphy has explained there will not be a catered meal at that evening's venue, the Denver Botanic Gardens. There, the band will play two sets in an outdoor amphitheater, while Maren helps Dennis Jeter sellout the last of his tee shirts, and when I understand how content she seems, smiling at prospective customers between sets, correcting Dennis on the way to fold a shirt, I leave the crowd and wander at sunset away from the stage toward the nearby flowers and trees, water running in the pool of the spacious Japanese Garden area, birdsong mingling there with the music that I can still hear from afar. A plane flies over. By another pond in an area called the Monet Garden, where, appropriately, water lilies have opened, the rock I sit on is still warm from the afternoon sun; two kids with bare feet test the water and a bird swoops in for a drink; drinks; stands still; drink again; flies off.

In a dream last night, I was traveling not with Maren but with *the happiest family* as my father used to call us, and I was sure, looking out the window, that we were going in the wrong direction.

"Hans," my mother exclaimed. "Hans. This isn't the way."

Dad kept on driving. He was smoking one of his cigars. The smoke from the cigar filled the car, but no one said, "Put it out." We were used to it.

"Dad," my brother piped up. "Mom's right. This isn't the way home."

Our father had stopped talking. He seemed very intent on the road. The car began to accelerate. Where were we? Why was he doing this?

At a corner we'd come to, the car stopped. My heart was beating fast, I looked at my brother and sister next to me, our mother in the seat by our father in the front, and I opened the door.

"Come on," I said to my brother and sister. "Get out."

They followed me to the curb.

"What are you doing?" our father said, raising his voice. But he stayed in the car. Our mother had now joined us on the side of the road. We were holding hands, the four of us, staring at Dad.

Then the light changed and the car left without us. It soon disappeared in the dusk as we watched. Then we began walking slowly in the other direction. No one said anything for the longest time. We never saw Dad again.

Thinking of him now, as I remain as if in a trance on the rock by the garden pond, I see him at the organ at Easter, I see a thousand people in the church turn their heads as he begins the breathtaking arpeggios of the Widor Toccata; soon the brass enter, and the moment comes when, with full organ, he ascends to a climax so loud and powerful that some in the congregation have to cover their ears.

The church is empty another day at dinner time, when my brother and I find him unconscious in the choir loft. Cradling his head in my lap, I try to make a joke about the accommodations, while my brother shuts off the organ and turns out the light on the console.

I see myself talking with him on the front porch, a hot night long ago in mid-September, and there are tears in his eyes as he says to me his brother's name, over and over, and the next day we fly to Boston, where he is admitted to Massachusetts General Hospital and sedated with a drug that makes him slur his speech and stumble when he walks. Later, he lies in a hospital bed, unshaven, wearing a white gown, his hair mussed, tubes connected to various parts of his aging body.

"You're going to be fine, Pop," I say.

"No," he answers, "I'm not."

For a family as vested as ours in the ritual and rhythm of religion, we made few attempts to get God working actively on our side, even at such moments of supreme crisis. Most of what passed for prayer in our household consisted of grace before dinner and, while we children were young, a devotional song that was sung with our mother before bed. My father never participated in those nightly proceedings, perhaps because he believed that, like giving us baths and reading us stories, they were not his "department." But he took an inordinate interest in our activities; a day never passed when he did not ask us about school, our music lessons, our friends. He was terribly proud of us, and we went everywhere with him: not only to the church when he practiced but to stores when he ran errands for our mother, to the homes of friends whom he called on as though he were a clergyman. If a member of the church were sick or had just lost a relative, my father was there to comfort them, and I often went along, listening all the way over as my father described their situation in melodramatic terms. I remember when two sons of someone in the church were killed in an automobile crash; driving by their home later on, my father would repeat the story of what had happened and wonder aloud how that family found the strength to go on. When one of my best childhood friends killed himself while we were in college, my father called to tell me and later, since I could not come home for the funeral, called again to report on the service. He said he played the hymn, *Be Still My Soul*, to the tune of the main theme from *Finlandia*. My friend's grandmother had requested it, he had told me.

"That was a tough one," he continued, almost as if he were referring to himself rather than the family of my friend.

Speaking with my mother shortly after he died, I recalled the parties she and my father used to throw, occasions when she would cook for 16 to 20 people and, an extravagance, someone would come in to serve the food and help with the cleanup.

"Do you remember the hat party?" she asked. Guests had to wear hats representing puns on the titles of musical compositions.

"Yes," I answered. "Dad's hat was a bottle of club soda wrapped in blue cloth. *Rhapsody in Blue.*"

As we spoke, disparate images came to my mind: the parking lot at Sears where we used to buy our Christmas trees, the undertaker's office in Tryon and the crematorium in the rear, with a chimney rising up through the roof.

I've told Maren many of these stories about her grandfather. She usually just listens, or she'll remind me sometimes that what I've started to say she's heard before. I've told her about my friend who shot himself, the motel he checked into after the holidays when we were in college, the incredibly sad visit I made to see his parents afterwards. I've told her about another childhood friend whose father died suddenly of a heart attack just a few weeks before we started high school. I've told her, too, about the widow of a civil rights martyr I met in Mississippi, how her home was firebombed by the Klu Klux Klan one night and her husband's last word before he died was his wife's name: Jewel. I've told her about a Native American woman I first met when I was a teenager, doing volunteer work in North Dakota, and how this woman's home and the homes of many of her friends were taken by the government when she was a child and flooded as part of a project to build a huge dam on the Missouri River.

I remembered a night in Northampton when I thought I'd see if a coffee house a friend runs was open but I got there too late, kept driving and parked my car in a lot behind Main Street, had the radio on, the local jazz program was having a Miles Davis night, sat in my parked car for a moment and listened to the end of *So What*, became aware as I sat there of a woman in what must have been the back of an apartment closing the blinds in her room, watched as the light in another window went dark, locked my car and walked through an alleyway to Main Street, which I crossed, and then continued walking around the corner of the office building adjacent to City Hall and stopped finally by the first-floor office where my mother once worked for the city's Council of Aging, retiring not long before she moved, the office was on the side of the building that looked out on a small park toward an old theater where my older daughter used to dance in the *Nutcracker* every Christmas, Maren was also in the production one year as a reindeer, I used to meet my mother for movies there, too…and then I walked back toward my car, decided on impulse to see if the Iron Horse was open, walked toward it in the dark and knew as I neared it from the quiet outside its entrance that it was closed, kept walking anyway and stopped, finally, at the huge window behind its stage, remembering how I'd stood at this very spot waiting in line to get into the club the first night I'd come to hear Wynton play, before my travels began, and I peered into the window on this dark night, looking and listening for ghosts, as if by some mysterious mental alchemy I could bring back the past, not permanently and certainly not all of it but selected moments: a dinner my mother invited us to at her apartment after one of Christian's soccer games, this must have been in October when he was in fourth or fifth grade, when he played on a team that the father of one his school friends coached, the game would have started around four in the afternoon so it would have been dark by the time it was over and we got to my mother's, where she had set the table festively, even putting out candles, and Christian must have helped her in the kitchen while Anna drew pictures on the floor and my wife nursed Maren, who was still a baby; it is so warm from the oven in my mother's small apartment that she has opened the door to the front patio where she got her mail and liked to sit on nice days, reading and listening to music from the stereo she could hear through an open window, and how...how...I ask myself as I stand by the darkened window of this club where I met this musician whom I would follow around the world only to discover that what I found I already knew...how could I ever summon again that moment with my mother, which was only one moment of so many...to say to her as I held her withered, precious hand with the wedding ring she would always wear on her fourth finger that there was really nothing else in the world I would rather have or do than to be there in that apartment once more, waiting for us all to take our seats at the table as her pot roast was served.

With the first cool air of evening, the music becomes louder as I walk back closer to where I started. Eric is in the midst of another virtuoso improvisation, this one on *Cherokee*, the speed breathtaking and somehow he has added a stride chorus that he will repeat in a different tune in a very different format several hours later. After midnight, in the midst of a long phone conversation from his hotel room regarding Jazz at Lincoln Center programming choices, Wynton receives a phone call from Eric, who with Walter and Carlos has traveled after the gig downtown to the oldest jazz club in the city, El Chapultepec.

"I'm coming," Wynton says to Eric, and then to me, "Swig, Maren can hang out here with the boys, they can watch a movie or play chess, Boss Murphy will check on them."

And we go, a taxi takes us, we get there the long way, driving by the new stadium where the Denver Broncos play and the old one where they used to play and finishing finally in a boisterous neighborhood right next to Coors Field, home of the Colorado Rockies, the construction of which has clearly triggered a commercial gentrification of the neighborhood with sports bars and grilles and discos all doing a booming business tonight even though the Rockies are out of town. But Chapultepec, at the corner of Market and 20th, looks like it hasn't changed in 50 years, the walls lined with photos of jazz artists and other musicians, the tables by the small bar packed with people of all ages, most of whom to judge from the air quality must be smokers, and a small band plays a blues by the doorway at the end of the bar, the door open, the lights low.

A slight stirring of recognition occurs amongst the intimate crowd as Wynton takes a seat at a table. Jerry the owner, with a cigarette dangling from his lips, asks Wynton what he'd like to drink.

"You have any cognac?" Wynton says. And Jerry brings him an enormous glass, from which Wynton takes just a sip before Jerry is at the front, saying there's a special guest in the house tonight and would you all please welcome...Wynton Marsalis! And Wynton begins playing with the combo that has been there all night, and then one by one his own musicians sit in, too, and it's a nice vibe here, nothing manic, no over-the-top would you believe b.s., and they keep playing until last call at two a.m., by which time two friends of Wynton's who happened to be there have offered us a ride back to the hotel, and we somehow all squeeze into a station wagon, one of the friends saying he'll sit on the floor of the rear luggage compartment. Our return route is through the city itself, along tree-lined streets and a neighborhood with large homes and then a few apartment buildings and then a business zone, this must be part of the area I watched from the window of Wynton's hotel suite before we left, a little sliver of an immense urban area, bounded by the mountains on its western side and the plains in every other direction, and the entire, invisible rest of the country beyond that jagged perimeter.

The next morning we put those plains

behind us and begin to climb these mountains. We are on our way to Aspen, where the band will play a kind of runout gig, leaving soon afterwards on a long trip to St. Louis, but first letting off Maren and me. My daughter and I will stay over with Denver friends one more day before flying home. To expedite our drop-off, and make it possible to stick with the band to and from Aspen, I've rented a car in which I trail the bus as it leaves Loews Denver Hotel and, inadvertently, makes a square loop around the vicinity until Kim figures out the location of the interstate's entrance. Then we go north, past downtown, before intersecting with I-70 west, before the turnoff for Boulder where the epic ride through that mountain snowstorm to Las Vegas with Harold Russell at the wheel began on what was a spring evening in Boulder, and we pass Golden where I was once startled to discover that rather than being nestled by the mountain stream pictured in television ads the imposing Coors brewery stands hard by a giant, paved parking lot, and we continue upward past Loveland Ski Area (closed for the season but still with lots of snow) to the Eisenhower Tunnel, where the road literally burrows through an otherwise impassable pathway to the other side of the Continental Divide.

Well before that landmark, I've left my rental car in the parking lot of a bank just off the highway in a small town in what are euphemistically called the foothills. Back on the bus, I interrupt a conversation Maren is having with Eric Lewis.

"Hey, sweetie, please help us remember this exit number when we come back tonight. Well, actually it will be early morning."

For a time, Wynton holds court up front, talking about Roy Eldridge, who he says taught him how to growl on the trumpet, and this brings up the general subject of music education. Wynton recalls a recent visit to Southern Methodist University in Texas, where he was a visiting lecturer for a week.

"Before I came the students learned *Blood on the Fields*," he says of his Pulitzer Prize winning piece that even his own band, since an international tour after the prize was announced in 1997, does not perform. "It brought tears to my eyes."

An achievement like that, Wynton continues--meaning what those students did--doesn't come about automatically. "You have to make it happen," Wynton says, and now of course he could be referring to himself but he doesn't say so.

Carlos again brings up a recurrent question about the band's ability to make music happen without tension in the rhythm section over such basic matters as the beat. Wynton recalls various combinations of players in his original septet that did and didn't work well, and then he mentions his brother Branford.

"When we were young, playing together, it was almost as if we were one horn," Wynton says, with matter-of-fact pride that sounds more sentimental than boastful, though Wynton has often resolutely insisted he is never nostalgic.

"You sound better now," Wynton continues, laughing, and referring not just to Carlos but to the entire rhythm section. But anyway, he adds boisterously, "you can't mess with what I'm dealing with."

Absent-mindedly, I've been keeping an eye out the window while listening to the conversation around me. My cell phone rings, surprising me—I didn't think it would work up here.

"Where are you?" a friend from back east asks.

"Let me look," I reply, and instantly realize we've made another wrong turn. We're off the interstate, on the road south to Leadville, an old mining town, beyond which is a shortcut to Aspen—if you're in a car with good snow tires and maybe a set of chains just in case.

Four summers ago I was in a vehicle that took that shortcut, by mistake, and almost didn't make it. I was on my way to the same jazz festival we're heading to now, in a Winnebago with Wynton and Frank Stewart and a new driver named Keith. We'd just driven all the way from New York City in less than 48 hours, with a stop in Nebraska to watch a basketball playoff game on television, and we were meeting Wynton's big band at the Silvertree Hotel in Snowmass Village at Aspen, same destination as today, except that time we were going to be staying at Snowmass for a couple of days while Wynton rehearsed the band before it began a western tour. When Keith reached the point where the shortcut crossed Independence Pass the road was covered with snow—this was in June, too.

"Keep your eye on the yellow line," Wynton said that day to Keith.

"There is no yellow line," Keith had replied.

Now, outside Leadville, I say something to Boss Murphy, who immediately goes to Kim and whispers and Kim pulls over and calls the Silvertree on his cell phone. My interference isn't a matter of etiquette but of life and death; were we to head up the narrow road to Independence Pass there would be no room to turn around and a reasonably good chance the bus would slip off the pavement, tip over, and fall several thousand feet down a mountain slope.

Four years ago I was on the Winnebago

with Wynton because he had committed to finishing the book we had started a decade earlier in Boston. I had with me a copy of the manuscript filled with comments from our new editor, whom Wynton had just met a month earlier in New York. We were in western Pennsylvania or eastern Ohio, several hours after leaving the city, before I'd opened the box with the edited manuscript and spread out its pages on the Winnebago's dining table.

"Where's the part we wrote that time in London?" Wynton asked, meaning what was then a prologue in his voice that began, *I like the late-night sound of the train*. We'd worked on that passage in the café of a London hotel and then again in a hotel room in Nice: *On the road, something incredible can take place at any moment, something that can reaffirm or realign your conception of who you are and want to be in the world*. These words had been moved to the end of the edited manuscript.

"Why did you do that, Swig?"

"I thought they worked better there, as a coda."

"They're not a coda. They're a prologue."

"Well, we can always move them back to the beginning."

"Uh-huh. What else you got there?"

And I started to read some of the editorial

comments.

"Let me ask you something, Swig. I've been out on the road all these years, and you've come out with us to all these gigs, we're on our way to another one right now, and someone who's never been with us, I'm sure she's a wonderful person and all and I'm glad to know she loves the music, but you mean to tell me that we're going to change all sorts of things in our book because she thinks we should? Who's book is this?"

I put the manuscript pages away and we never looked at them again on that trip.

Now, Kim isn't happy about having to turn around, and neither is anyone else on the bus because it means we have lost whatever opportunity there might be for a soundcheck or a hotel nap. We aren't back on I-70 for long before we have to pull off again, this time because the treads on one of the tires for the trailer the bus is pulling has burned off. It's late in the afternoon before we finally reach the Aspen/Snowmass fork in the road where we take the turn to the Silvertree, all the way at the end of the road, the hotel built right into the bottom of the Snowmass ski slopes, with an ersatz village surrounding it, and kids who are attending the resort's Suzuki music camp walk around carrying violins.

*

Maren and I have no hotel room for this brief visit, and so we leave our stuff on the bus. When I was here before, the festival took place in an open field just down the road from the hotel, but this year it has been moved to a tent in Aspen itself, several miles away. So we still have another ride ahead of us, after the band members have showered and changed. Rob is going ahead now, to check on the sound system, but I remember the shops in the village and am pretty sure they will still be open.

I follow Maren around the side of the hotel that faces a chairlift and ask her to stop by one of the lift towers.

"Why?"

"I want to take your picture."

"Oh, Dad, that's so corny." And she keeps walking downhill, toward the level where the shops are. So in the photograph I take you just see her from the rear, wearing maroon pants and a white tee shirt over a long-sleeved tan turtleneck, her black purse dangling from her right shoulder, and swaying from her head long locks of her reddish-brown hair that she had cut and colored before we left on this trip, and she seems to be leaning with the angle of the hair, as if she were moving to some music she could hear in her head, and beyond her in the photograph are the slopes of other mountains forming a green valley, the early evening sky still blue with white wisps of clouds.

Maren quickly finds a boutique that sells jewelry and "stuff" and starts looking at earrings for her pierced ears. We are the only people in the store other than the shopkeeper, a beautiful, blond-haired woman who introduces herself as Cyndi. She's deeply tanned and smiles constantly as she talks a little about herself, tells us she loves the snow but doesn't ski much anymore, says she used to date a comedian and travel a lot, is a Barbra Streisand fan and did we know Vince Gill, he stopped by the store just the other day.

"Why don't you pick out a bracelet," I say to Maren. "To remember our trip."

Cyndi helps her select something simple and gives us a deep discount on it. Maren leaves the store wearing the new bracelet, and we meet the band at the hotel lobby door and ride to the gig in a large van. It's almost dark by the time we get there, and while the band is being introduced we're invited to help ourselves to food in the commissary tent for festival employees. We listen to some of the music from behind the stage and then walk around its edge, near one side of the enormous tent, where an usher lets us through a temporary gate. Another, smaller tent stands adjacent to the main one, and I discover that our backstage passes permit us to enter this tent as well, where gourmet food and fine wines are being served to festival donors. I enjoy a glass of a California cab while Maren scarfs down some strawberry shortcake, and then I help myself to a second glass of wine and take it back with me as we find seats in the main tent.

"Can I have a sip?" Maren whispers.

"Sure," I say. "To a great week. I love you."

She squeezes my chilly hand; it's cold up here in the mountains at night.

"Love you, too."

Maren knows from much experience that one place not to get lost is backstage after a gig if you need a ride. And so she stays near me, while I keep Wynton in my line of vision. He seems in no particular hurry to be leaving, but I know from my experience that when he's ready to go somewhere he goes, and if you don't follow along right away you'll be left behind. You could be one of his sons and he wouldn't wait for you (though he would, if you were one of those boys, be certain to ask someone to stick with you). Sure enough, just as he finishes a plate of food someone on the festival staff saved for him, he stands up, grabs his trumpet, and more or less bolts in the direction of the backstage exit. I run after him, and Maren runs after me.

By pure chance, no one else in the band leaves just then, and we end up together, the three of us, in the seat right behind the driver in an otherwise empty van. Maren sits between us, and we ride together back to the Silvertree. Wynton quickly starts a conversation with the driver, who tells us he lives in Las Vegas, where he works as a bartender, and is just helping out a buddy tonight by doing this driving while he visits for a few days.

"That was beautiful, what Eric did tonight on *Magic Hour*," I say. "I like how you've been letting him just end the piece himself, that lullaby."

Wynton sort of nods and mumbles some kind of "uh-huh" and asks Maren does she have enough room and, "I'm sorry we didn't get to spend more time together, you'll have to come to New York with your dad," and then, to me, "How did the band sound?" by which I assume he means in part how did it sound with Herlin Riley playing the drums tonight, Ali having left last night for a weekend gig at the Village Vanguard and Wynton's regular big band drummer and original septet member Herlin having flown in from New Orleans for this gig and the one to come in St. Louis.

"Nothing has meaning on its own," Wynton suddenly declaims. "You have to *give* it meaning, invest it with life. Another day in the world, we played a gig, and now we go home."

Or, in this case, back to the hotel, where the bus will be leaving in about an hour.

"You don't have a room?" Wynton says as we walk him to his. "Stay here."

Maren parks herself in front of a television and I follow Wynton into the next room, where the television was never turned off earlier. Wynton sits down and in silence we watch a few minutes of *Sportscenter*, then his cell phone rings and he disappears into the bathroom for a minute, comes out wearing jeans and a blue work shirt, and, still talking on his phone through a headpiece, sits down again, clicks the off button on the phone, sighs, looks past my shoulder into the room where Maren is now reading a magazine, shakes his head and smiles.

"This is what life will always be," he says without any prompting. "What it is. They eat great meals, they marry their old ladies, they make love, they blow into horns...but they have to blow beauty into them, into life. And then they die. We're just like the Romans hanging out two thousand years ago, Swig. Yass, yass."

Then he stands and without another word walks into the next room and starts to talk with Maren, says something to her about pimps and drug dealers but I can't really hear the conversation and don't try, try only to stay awake until we're on the bus again, where Kim thinks it will be about five a.m. or so when we reach the place where I left our rental car and so I wander to the back lounge, set the alarm on my phone for 4:30, and fall asleep before the bus begins to move.

The sound of that alarm a few hours later startles me. I collect my things and walk back through the darkened bunk area, poke Maren in hers, and find Wynton, Carlos, and Eric in the front of the bus, deep in a continuation of the conversation about staying together on the bandstand that began in Los Angeles. It's still dark out.

"Got a ways to go," Kim says, and I take a seat near him, drift in and out of the talk around me, watch the road, nod off, and then, "We're here," Kim is saying. I'd fallen to sleep again and I stand now and walk back to Maren's bunk and wake her again, too, and by then Kim has the bus idling by our car, and he opens the luggage door underneath and I find our stuff and put it in the trunk of the car.

"Well, goodbye," Maren is saying inside. "Thank you so much."

"What, you don't have any hugs for us," Carlos deadpans.

Maren blushes, smiles, hugs Carlos, hugs

Eric, and looks at Wynton, who pretends for a second like he's never met her. Then he does one of his whoops, laughs again, smiles, throws his arms around her and says, "I love you, girl. You take good care of that old dad of yours." And we get off the bus.

Kim waits while I start the car, and not until I wave, signaling that we are fine, does he put the bus in motion. It's light enough to see now, the sun just coming up far off to our east, over the plains. The clock in the Camry flashes 5:15. Across the lot an old guy appears out of nowhere, must live down the street, he and his dog on their morning walk.

"Dad," Maren says. "Are we going?"

"In just a minute, Maren," I reply, not moving, and I wait while I watch Wynton's bus exit the lot, listening to its gears grinding, then the sound of its wheels as it disappears beyond some trees, and I think of the men on board, in motion like the music they make, and I think again of D.J., Sally, Wess and Monyure; Wynton's housekeeper Anna Castillo from Honduras, how she always finds some food for me if I drop in and he's not there, Anna who takes the train everyday from the Bronx with her young son, whom she drops off at school after the hour-and-a-half ride before she starts work.

"Dad, I'm so tired. Can we please just go? Please?"

And so we do, leaving the lot a few minutes after the bus, which when we get back onto the interstate has disappeared from view. Sitting in the seat beside me, Maren seems already to be asleep.

"Will the radio bother you?" I ask.

No response.

Hitting the scan button, I find a jazz station, and I turn the volume up a little. Maren doesn't stir.

I remember the day I almost missed my ride to the airport. I was using a van service that trip and when the driver rang the bell at the house we were renting after selling the farmhouse I was still asleep. It was 4:30 a.m. and he had other people in the van already he told me. "How many minutes do I have?" I asked. "Five," he replied and meant it.

Funny, I think that was the time we were all convening in Denver and then onto Fort Collins, and from there it was a short drive the next day to Wyoming, where I went on that walk in Laramie the following morning with Harold Russell and Darlene, before we left for Cheyenne.

There's a Charlie Parker tune playing on the car radio. Funny, the first time I was in New Orleans with Wynton, one night we went to get something to eat at a Chinese place near the tree-lined street where his parents lived. Wynton's oldest son was along, age three or four at the time, and Dr. Michael White, a New Orleans native who taught Spanish literature at Xavier University, where Wynton with his band and Michael had spent that day learning some King Oliver tunes. At the Chinese place Michael and Wynton had started talking about Sidney Bechet and I didn't know who that was.

"Don't matter," Wynton had said kindly. "I didn't used to know either."

That first tour for me had commenced right after we'd moved from the farm into the rented ranch house, which came with an enormous attached garage into which we more or less dumped all the stuff from the move that we didn't know what to do with. This happened in July, during a hot spell. On our final day at the farm I had walked through the farmhouse one last time, its empty rooms already giving off a mustiness in the heat, and my footsteps had reverberated in the front hallway as I climbed its slippery wooden stairway.

At the top of the stairway, around the corner of the balustrade, there was a tiny room with two windows that looked out at the gentle valley below the house. For a time I had a desk there, but when Maren was born we made it her bedroom, the crib in the corner formed where the wall of our bedroom met the front of the house, above the porch. I looked in there that last afternoon, then slowly walked back through the hallway, past the other bedrooms and the upstairs bath with the Victorian bathtub we'd never replaced, and into the rear upstairs of the farmhouse that originally must have been where the hired hand lived. Except for one room I'd used as a study, we never got around to fixing this part of the house, though we had enclosed the hole at the end where the house used to meet the enormous barn, which we'd had torn down, partly because it was a fire hazard and partly because the expense of renovating it would have been so high. I stared out the back window to the ball field with the homemade backstop where Christian and I had played every night after supper, and then I walked down the back stairs, outside, where our children were waiting somewhat impatiently for us to get going. Having long before purchased a ticket to a summer dance performance, Bonnie had already driven off, leaving me to take the kids to our new place, which was only about half an hour away. Two or three days later I got on a plane for New Orleans.

"Dad?" Maren's voice startles me. I was sure she was fast asleep. "We almost there?"

"There" is my friends' house, where we have instructions to let ourselves in so we don't wake anyone up, though I have a feeling that someone will be waiting. We've turned off I-70 now, past the exit for Boulder to the north, and we're traveling south on I-25, actually the same road we were on two days earlier from New Mexico, the reverse of the route Wynton and I followed in that taxi the other night when he played at Chapultepec.

"I know that tune," I think, half listening to the radio, and then, "Yes, it's the first cut on *the Marciac Suite*," the piece Wynton wrote in 1999 for the small town in southwestern France where he's been attending the jazz festival every summer. I first heard this tune five summers ago, when Maren was 10, and a band that was composed partly of Wynton's old septet, augmented by a few more musicians, played a five-night engagement at the Iron Horse, two sets a night, every set a sellout.

Maren and Bonnie came to the club one night and Maren, age 10, helped me take notes during part of the performance. "Pretty tune," she wrote in her stylish cursive. "Bluezy jazz." The rest of her notes are similarly cryptic, just little phrases:

Joking around.
Wintin's playing,
everyone joins
quick, mellow tone
and, upbeat!

breaking into
sudden stop
talking
Herlin fools around —
on drums

We were no longer living in the rented house then, but I could never forget that first fall there when the band came to Amherst for a gig at the nearby state university, and after soundcheck Wynton accepted my invitation to drive by and say hello to my family. Bonnie had thought we were going out and when we surprised her she was serving the kids supper. Wynton confessed he was hungry, and the only thing Bonnie had made because it was all we had in the house that evening was Campbell's Chicken Noodle soup with grilled cheese sandwiches. Wynton said how good it tasted and gave everyone a hug when he left,

Maren was only three years old then, Maren who came home from the hospital after her birth on a cold January morning, wrapped in red bunting and a pink hooded sweater knit by her mother, who held her in her arms outside the hospital with our other two children standing by her, Anna gripping in one small hand the pink roses my mother had given her new granddaughter, and we drove home together that day, the five of us, back to our house on the hill, my family whom I later left all those mornings when I went on the road, and you never knew, could not know if you'd see the sun in the morning, "Will I See the Sun in the Morning Blues," sing them now, *Oh the memories that music marries, the voices of pain and joy that love leaves in our lives.*

V
Ricochet

Coming from Cardiff into London, Wynton dozed in the backseat of a Mercedes driven by an engaging, loquacious Welsh chauffeur named Roger, who freely dispensed geographic and linguistic information about his ancient homeland, rhapsodized about the quality of his automobile, which he proudly said he had traveled to Germany to pick up, and shared stories about previous clients, including Stephen Sondheim, whom he praised for his intelligence and thoughtfulness. That name got a rise out of Wynton.

"Yeah," Wynton said. "He's *great*."

"Ran into the maestro yesterday morning at breakfast," I said. "'And what brings you here?' he asked, and I said something about the continuing challenge of getting on paper this elusive art, and I mentioned the gig on Friday in Birmingham. 'Yes,' Mr. Masur said, 'it is history.' Skain, you listening?"

"I'm here," he said, looking up from a paperback book of math puzzles he was studying. "Kurt Masur," Wynton added. This was the highest form of a compliment he paid: to say someone's name, just the name.

In Birmingham, Wynton had stayed late after the gig for an interview. Some fans had wanted to see him, too, a crowd of them by the stage door in the lobby of the atrium attached to the magnificent hall. Two were university students I had overheard as I was scribbling notes after the second encore, amazed, I heard one of them say, "to be standing by the expensive seats." I was able to get them backstage, where they had waited it must have been an hour, and when Wynton finally came through the doorway the words tumbled out of their mouths.

"Thank you, thank you," they exclaimed, and, "Did you hear me shout, 'Alleluia?'"

Now, we could see the water of Bristol Bay as we left Wales, somewhere past a sign for some Roman ruins. It was a cool, misty Sunday morning, the landscape green. Nearing London after a stop at a fast-food place for breakfast, I recognized the streets near Heathrow, not far from Windsor Castle, and remembered when I flew over here in '92, the time Wynton and I worked together on the "late night sound of the train" section of our book in the coffee shop of the hotel near Wellington Arch, started writing it actually, finished it in Nice.

Bonnie had driven me to Bradley airport for that trip, and because this was long before 9/11 she could walk me to the gate. Maren was along, too, still a toddler. I took one of those small prop planes on a connection to Boston where I was getting my London flight, and I remembered now, in Roger's Mercedes, the sight of my wife and very young daughter waving to me as the plane left the gate. There was something in that moment I had been fighting ever since, as if I were afraid of its power. "Going," I had such conflicted feelings, because I was certain as well that I was also actually "coming."

Quiet, calm streets as we entered London now, less than three months removed from the terrorist bombings in the city's subway system. What did he as an American citizen make of the war in Iraq? Roger had asked Wynton, tentative in his introduction of the subject, not wishing to provoke but nevertheless curious—and, it was clear from the way he himself spoke about Prime Minister Blair, deeply troubled. Wynton had responded immediately and emphatically with a stream of profanity, howling expletives directed at the incompetence and coldness of America's political leadership, shockingly on prominent display in the pathetic response to Katrina as well.

Just before we reached our hotel we passed Holland Park, and I recognized its name, remembered that was where my parents lived for several months when my dad had some kind of fellowship and a leave from his church. It was right after I was married, my wife and I living in a walkup in Providence, Rhode Island, while she finished college and I taught at a small public school. I remembered how filled with expectation my father was when they returned that winter; we met them at Logan Airport, went out to eat somewhere, and he talked glowingly about the future without once saying anything about the present.

There would be more of what my father invariably referred to in his letters as "new days." Right up to the morning that my mother drove him from the Berkshires to the airport in Albany, I think he somehow thought she would join him in North Carolina. Even after she had moved to Northampton, he was still writing her, begging her to change her mind, but by then she was beginning what became after much anguish a new life for herself, and for us.

I had been thinking about my mother during the last encore in Birmingham, when Wynton played *Embraceable You*. Though she loved best the Rodgers and Hammerstein she used to sing with my father accompanying on the piano, my mother used to perform Gershwin, too. Having been invited after prolonged applause to the front of the stage by the maestro, who stood off to one corner, his hands at his sides, his body motionless, Wynton by turns soft and loud, high and low, always clear, cutting the air around him, then caressing it, *became* the music, which in turn became the comfort to someone's sorrow, the celebration of another's happiness, even or perhaps especially the other musicians also still on stage, who listened with a rare attentiveness if not awe.

Taking the train from London's Gatwick Airport up to Birmingham on the day of the concert there, I had gazed out the window at the farms we passed, people on the platforms at stations we sped through, rain on the streets and on the spires of Coventry Cathedral, which was bombed in World War II and then partially rebuilt. As I looked out from my hotel window the following morning, at what I could see of the old industrial city, and with the music from the night before still playing in my head, I thought also about my daughter and how she sounded when I called her before my plane left, the hope I heard in her voice. She'd finished her sophomore year of high school on the honor roll and over the summer had worked extra hours at the bakery where she'd been employed part-time, on and off, since eighth grade. She'd passed a very difficult figure-skating test and was, she said, "taking a break" from that longtime activity. She had learned to drive and earned her license on the first try, something she was very proud of.

Roger dropped us off at our London hotel with good wishes for the concert, which he regretted he would miss, he told Wynton, "but I hope to attend the one in Scotland," he said. Leaving tomorrow morning, I'd be home by then; tonight was my last gig.

My room wasn't ready, but Wynton invited me to share his while I was waiting. He also loaned me his cell phone, because it had an international connection, so I could call my family. There was a Billie Holiday tune he wanted me to hear, and he repeatedly played one phrase, *And when we want to dance, we dance*. Smiling, he sang the line himself as he hit the button on his remote to go back to it again.

"See what she does there, how the whole vibe changes," he said. Then he played it once more.

The hotel phone rang and Wynton took the call. I left him and used his cell phone to make another call. When I was finished I could not hear anything from his room, so I poked my head in. Wynton, it appeared, had fallen asleep.

"What you saying, Swig?" he said, without opening his eyes.

"I traveled with you all over the world to hear this music before I understood it didn't matter where I was."

"Yes...yes," Wynton said. "I keep trying to tell the cats, the music's internal."

"Well, I don't think you can teach someone that, I mean by telling them. They have to discover it...Anyway, I thought I'd go check if my room's ready. I'll see you later."

Clearing, the London sky had invited the sun to make a rare appearance that afternoon, and around four o'clock, after a solitary lunch at an Italian place around the corner from the hotel, I decided to walk to Royal Albert Hall, where the chorus, augmented by additional singers for a performance in such a large space, was supposed to be having a pre-concert rehearsal with the composer. But when I arrived at the legendary venue the chorus was singing without Wynton--without orchestra or jazz band, too; the only accompaniment was from a piano, played by one of the singers who was reading off a roughly transcribed reduction of the instrumental parts. I took a seat near the stage, where one of the orchestra's percussionists was setting up the array of instruments she would be playing during the performance, and then I wandered out into the main lobby, separated from the auditorium by a carpeted hallway lined with photographs of past performers: Elton John; Liza Minelli; Rudolf Nureyev.

Through a glass doorway I could see across the street a restored monument to Prince Albert. The late light reflected off the gilded statue of the prince and the surrounding ornamentation.

I walked up a flight of marble stairs, where another lobby led to another set of stairs. I kept climbing, level by level, until I had reached the last, which opened up to a near ceiling-height area that all but encircled the perimeter of the huge hall. Wynton, I observed from my high perch, had at last arrived at the rehearsal. I followed along the rotunda-like walkway until I reached a kind of balustrade that prevented me from continuing around to what would have been the upper rear of the stage. From this spot I could see and hear the singers right below. Wynton had immediately gone to work with them on the a cappela section he had added after the New York premiere of the work, when *All Rise* had been a millennium commission of the New York Philharmonic. Then he moved to the climax.

"*Zum...Zum...*It's got to have a sound to it like a rattlesnake who just bit you, it's got to catch our attention," he said. Each time he stopped the chorus with another comment, he used some kind of similar analogy to make his point. He smiled when the chorus got it right, sort of shook his head and sighed when there was a mistake. He was dressed in a suit, not the one in which he would perform in a couple of hours, after a hurried meal in his dressing room, where he also gave a young boy a pre-concert trumpet lesson, but certainly something appropriate if he were making a presentation somewhere, meeting the Queen perhaps.

*Look beyond, look beyond, higher. Look higher, look higher and higher...*As the music echoed in the vast expanse of Royal Albert Hall, I heard within myself a different note, far off and then closer, like a voice coming from a well, and then other notes, coming toward me and then through me, off me, as if the sound were an actual thing, not simply resounding but rebounding. With my eyes closed I tried to see the source of the sound, but only the reflection of my eyes stared back at me, or so it seemed.

I wasn't there, of course, but when my parents lived those several months long ago in Holland Park, my father had talked his way into trying the Royal Albert Hall organ, the pipes of which now formed a backdrop to the scene before me. It was my mother who told me about this years later. She and whoever let them in were the only other people in the building when he played some Bach, a little Franck, maybe some Buxtehude, she thought but couldn't remember.

I closed my eyes again, imagining that moment. Once he was at the organ bench, it was as if nothing else in his life really existed, let alone mattered. All the things he could not control in his life—lack of money, lack of authority, his children's ambitions, his wife's needs, his friends' demands—were put in abeyance, subservient to the seduction of those black and white keys and the magical buttons and knobs called stops that in an instant could change the sound of a note from flute, say, to trumpet. At the girls' school where my father taught music after he resigned his post at the Buffalo orchestra, his students used to call him Uncle Hans, still called him that when they had grown up and, getting married, asked him to play the music at their weddings. There was one march in particular, something he had written himself, that most of them requested. Had he played it, too, that day here in Royal Albert Hall?

As the chorus below me continued its rehearsal, I heard in my memory the notes of that march. With my eyes still closed, I saw the beginning of what I hoped was a smile on my father's gentle face. How I wished I had been able to reach out and touch that face a last time, after he fell that distant August night in North Carolina. Stern, his eyes were no longer light blue but green, then black like a thundercloud before a storm, followed finally by forgiving gray and then, once again, a tender blue. Suddenly all color left them, they were white, there was an intense white light obliterating everything…And now in my head I heard his voice calling my name from somewhere down in this very deep well, a long way down—a long way down from this high balcony where I stood. I imagined that depth as part of a line, in the way generations stand under or behind other generations, and when finally I opened my moist eyes, I felt momentarily dizzy and fell to my knees, had to use my hands to break the fall…*Look higher, look higher and higher*…And I said to myself, "How lucky I am! Now, at last, let me use these hands to make something, the ricochet of his ambition, accomplishment, heartbreak, and love, to share the feeling of what he heard that was beautiful, not somehow but triumphantly."

Epilogue

A year had passed, and I was in New York for a meeting and called Wynton afterwards.

"Come by in fifteen minutes, I won't be home long," Wynton said, and so I kept walking to his apartment, crossed the plaza that I had crossed on my way to or from countless concerts and rehearsals. The doorman whom I know let me go up the elevator to Wynton's floor. Not until I knocked did I realize Wynton had been saying to me he was not there yet but would be--but only for a short time because he had a date with someone. And so I waited in the hallway, my knocking on the door triggering an older man's opening his own door a few apartments around the hall corner, and he offered to call downstairs to the doorman who informed us Wynton was on his way.

"Swiginski," or something like that was the new variant on my nickname, and then, "hold on a minute." And so I went to the piano where I found a score of his on a shelf filled with scores, his own mixed with others, mostly Bach, and opened to the place near the end of the piece where the band starts a syncopated clap that audiences at premieres in Spain and Italy and Cleveland, Ohio have picked up in their applause. I sightread the chord structure on the piano, and then he emerged and lay down on the bed in his bedroom, called my name, we talked for a minute, I mentioned something about the Gershwin encore he had played at a recent gig in Pennsylvania, said, "Let me get some of those grapes in the kitchen," came back to the room and thought he had fallen asleep. Wouldn't have been the first time.

"What you doing, Swig?"

"I was going to read something, but I can see you're tired."

"No, please read."

So I started reading and at one point I was quite sure because he was snoring that he was in fact asleep, but I kept reading. And just when I was positive he was asleep I realized from the way he turned his head that he was listening to every word...

...We were on our way back from a gig in Troy, New York. It was a warm, spring evening, and the band was leaving by bus sometime after midnight on a long drive to Pittsburg. No longer touring regularly, I was about to drive home, just two hours away.

"Don't forget the sword," Wynton said to me after the gig. "It's the source of the music's power." Then his cell phone rang, , and we never finished the conversation...

...Standing up, Wynton said, "Hold on," and he called the restaurant where he was meeting whomever.

"Sorry, Swig, can you keep reading while I shave?"

"No prob, have done that before," and I picked up my reading...

... A few months later, mid-summer, I was in Maine to see my mother, who since several hospitalizations had been living there with my sister. En route afterwards to a friend's new house, where I would spend the night, I called Wynton from my car.

"So, what did you mean that time, when you started to talk about the sword?"

He paused for a moment, and I continued driving to my friend's, looking for the exit off I-295 that would take me towards Brunswick and then, with another turn, the ocean...

...Wynton was finished shaving and moved to his closet to iron a shirt. His assistant, perhaps the only person in the world who at any given moment might be able to answer a question about his whereabouts, called from his office. He told her I was there and we pretended to flirt through him. As sweet and caring as she was beautiful, she talked with him on the speakerphone while he continued to iron, and she mentioned a chorus she was singing with later.

"What time is it? I might come," he said to her. And then, to me, "I have to go, get your stuff."

I grabbed my black leather bag and in the hallway he made a stupid joke about how disrespectful I was not to have closed the door behind me properly and soon we were in the elevator.

"Where are you going?" he asked.

"Home," I answered. "I have my car here. Do you want a ride?"

He thought for a second as we walked outside.

"Thanks, but I should take a taxi. You want to ride along?"

I answered with my feet. We were at a corner on Broadway and, as if commanded, a taxi pulled up to let someone out and we got in and the driver, an older Black man, said, looking back, "Are you...Marsalis?" and Wynton of course said, "Yes, I am," and we started downtown and he urged me to continue...

..."*You know when someone or something has truly hurt you?*" Wynton said.

"*Yes.*"

"*So when that happens, you are completely vulnerable.*"

"*Yes.*"

"*But you must go on. So you create a kind of hardness around the hurt, to protect yourself, to face life."*

I listened.

"Music takes you there, takes you back to the place within you where you were hurt, takes you to that tenderness. That's the sword, because of where the music comes from."

At almost that exact moment in our conversation our cell phone connection started to breakup. We had been talking for about 30 seconds.

"I'll call you back," I said, but I never did, not then, not about that. ...

...Arriving at the restaurant, Wynton opened the door and reached for his wallet.

"No, I'll pay the man," I said. "I'm going to ask him to drive me right back to where we began."

"Okay," Wynton said, and got out and stood for a moment, looking at me through the window of the cab before it started moving again, waiting to catch my eye, and I looked, and he motioned with his arm and fist, up and down, a kind of variation on the old power salute. He did it a second time and I returned the gesture as he smiled, nodded his head, and disappeared.

Acknowledgments

Thank you: Edward C. Arrendell II, Joe Bills, Stephanie Bradford, DCE, David Foster, Hank, Bill Hart, Bernadette Horgan, Wayne S. Kabak, Phil Kass, Denis Laflamme, Christopher Muse, Phelicia, Rev. Robert L. Polk, Stuart Schoffman, Genevieve Stewart, Steve Strimer, Eric Suher, Kim Townsend, David Tripp, Christopher Vyce, Bruce Wilcox, Larry Williamson, and all the people who appear in the text.

www.ingramcontent.com/pod-product-compliance
Lightning Source LLC
LaVergne TN
LVHW041611070426
835507LV00008B/193